CIVIL WAR II

THE FALL OF AMERICA, BABYLON THE GREAT

STEVEN A. ALLEVATO

RoseDog Books

PITTSBURGH, PENNSYLVANIA 15238

RoseDog Books
585 Alpha Drive, Suite 103
Pittsburgh, PA 15238
Visit our website at www.rosedogbookstore.com

ISBN: 978-1-6495-7850-1
eISBN: 978-1-6495-7870-9

This book is dedicated to my mother
Deidre Allevato
RIP

ABOUT THE AUTHOR

STEVE ALLEVATO WAS BROUGHT TO THE 1991 Medjugorie Peace conference as a last resort by his mother, who was deeply troubled over his very severe addiction to crack cocaine.

Michael O'Brien, a vocalist at the conference, wrote Steve a note encouraging him to change his life so, he could be a witness to others.

Steve experienced a miraculous conversion and returned to the Lord and the Catholic Church.

Today, Steve teaches Catholic Apologetics and has been clean and sober for over 22 years.

By the grace of God, Steve is a successful Businessman, Lector, Rosary Prayer Group Leader and host of You-Tube Channel: "Catholic Apologetics for beginners."

While studying about the antichrist and the end of times for his apologetics class, Steve read the 18th chapter of the book of revelation.

While reading the chapter it seemed to be describing America.

A few years prior, Steve wrote notes about the possibility of a second civil war in America.

Steve wrote a rough draft of how a civil war could occur and thought, "Is it possible China could be responsible for the destruction of America?"

How could it occur?

Project Babylon.

While the manuscript was being written, some events described in the book were occurring on TV.

Are we on the brink?

Get some popcorn and enjoy "Civil War II: The Fall of America, Babylon the Great."

Steve does not advocate war or violence and prays for the conversion of America.

TABLE OF CONTENTS

CHAPTER 1

"THEY'RE READY FOR YOU, MISTER SHEPHERD," the aide said from the doorway of the backstage room where Marcus Shepherd was preparing for his rally. If he'd run four years ago, for the 2028 election, he would have been standing beside the stage the entire time, listening to the other speakers at the rally. With the rising tensions across the country, though, his secret service agents had insisted he be sheltered from the public as much as possible. A prudent precaution, Shepherd realized, though it irked him, too; these were his people. He shouldn't have to hide in fear from them.

"Thanks, Amy," Shepherd told his aide, nodding to the secret service agents posted at the door, who fell into step in front of and behind him as he began toward the stage. At least they were in Florida this week, a pleasant break from the January snows he'd been enduring at their rallies in the northern battleground states like Ohio and Michigan. The air was a bit chilly in just his suit jacket, but Shepherd was warmed by the roar of the crowd filling the area in front of the Tampa Convention Center, a roar that intensified as he mounted the steps of the stage and stepped up to the microphone. Republican nominee Shepherd watched the secret service securing the crowd perimeter as he waited for them to quiet enough for him to speak.

"My fellow Americans," Shepherd started, "For the past twelve years, I've fought tirelessly on the senate floor to restore our nation to its core values, making it a place all families can work, live, and worship in their own way. We've made great strides pushing back against the anti-religious policies of the liberal elite, returning to the moral center and personal freedom our great nation was founded on."

Shepherd paused for the crowd's resounding cheer, smiling out over the massive crowd. He saw no few children hoisted on their parents shoulders—a proud sight; the children were the future, as he'd always believed. It was heartening to see so many in attendance. When the cheers had hushed enough to go on, Shepherd said, "But we still have a lot of work to do. As I've outlined in my America First platform—"

A sudden sharp scream interrupted him. Shepherd cast his eyes about the crowd, saw a disturbance along the outer left edge; a flash of movement in his periphery and he turned to see one of his secret service agents crossing the stage quickly toward him, one hand to his ear-piece. More screams, sudden chaos, the crowd energy turning. Shepherd's eye caught a masked face, a crowbar in his hand, watched in terror as the masked man brought it down on the head of one of his supporters.

"What's happening?" he asked as the agent pulled him from the microphone, shuffling him off the stage.

"Leftist attack," the agent answered, shortly.

"How many?"

"At least twenty. All armed."

Shepherd tried to fight off the agent's grip—these were his people; he had to help them—but the agent grabbed harder, said, "Now, Mister Shepherd. You can't help them if you're dead."

And Marcus Shepherd knew—as much as he hated it—that he was right. The agent pulled Shepherd's suit jacket up over his head, blocking out his view of the crowd until all he could see were the swaying palm trees, their fronds[1] waving against the peaceful blue sky, a jarring dichotomy[2] to the screams echoing behind him.

---

[1] Frond – A large, finely divided leaf, especially those found on ferns and palms.
[2] Dichotomy – Mutually exclusive or contradictory events, thoughts, or actions.

✪ ✪ ✪

At his campaign offices in Los Angeles, California, Emmanuel Santos watched the news coverage of his rival's disastrous rally in Florida with growing unease. They'd interrupted CNBC's regular news programming a few hours before with breaking reports of the developing violence. The anchor in the newsroom cut away to a reporter on the ground outside the now-empty Tampa Convention Center. Behind him, sanitation workers were hosing the blood from the pavement, the wrecked stage listing to the side, its red, white, and blue streamers flapping sadly abandoned in the evening wind.

"I'm here at the Tampa Convention Center in Tampa Bay, Florida where earlier today a rally by Republican presidential hopeful Marcus Shepherd was interrupted by protestors," the reporter said. "Shepherd had just begun to speak when the protestors arrived. What started as a peaceful demonstration escalated quickly into violence when secret service agents attempted to dispel the protestors by force, in direct violation of their First Amendment rights. Four protestors were injured in the conflict, and many more are being held for questioning at the Hillsborough County Sherriff's Office. The protest was organized by the liberal action group Democratic Socialists[3] for American Freedom, which insists its aims at the rally were not to ferment[4] violence but simply to make their voices heard by the Republican establishment—"

Santos muted the television and looked around the room. Normally his offices were bustling with activity as his team prepared for the upcoming primaries, but it was evening, now, most of his staffers at home; only the core group remained in the chairs around him, watching the now-silent

---

[3] Socialism – Economic system based on distribution of power over industry, resources, and means of production to the community rather than to individuals. Democratic Socialism is a system of government in which basic services like health care and education are provided to citizens at little to no cost, but the government does not control all aspects of their operation and private property ownership is still allowed.

[4] Ferment - To cause agitation or excitement.

coverage with the same righteous indignation in their eyes that Santos felt in his core.

"Why do they always have to turn it violent?" his campaign manager, Mehar Ali, lamented from the chair beside him. "We have a right to have a voice. We're people, too."

"All the more reason we have to win in November," Santos answered. His staffers took the hint, drifting away from the television screen to go back to their desks and the work that awaited them there. That was one thing Santos respected about his people; they knew what needed to be done, no matter the hour or circumstance. And he wasn't going to let that hard work go to waste. Events like this only made him surer of his current path. If the other side was determined not to listen—well, then, they'd just have to speak louder. Make them hear. Emmanuel Santos drifted back to his own desk, rubbing his tired eyes in a futile attempt to stave off the headache blooming in his temples.

"Were there any casualties?" Marcus Shepherd asked. His running mate, Carol Moore, had just returned from a visit to Memorial Hospital. Shepherd had wanted to go himself. Those injured in the rally had come to see him; it was his responsibility to see to their safety, to reassure them that he could stop these senseless attacks. But the secret service had forbidden it. Too much risk, they said. What a terrible world, where a presidential candidate would put his life at risk simply visiting a hospital.

"Three dead," Carol answered, somberly. She was a strong woman, he knew, but her eyes were red-rimmed. And no shame in that; he wouldn't trust anyone who could feel good in the aftermath of such a senseless tragedy. She settled down next to him on the sofa in his hotel suite and said, "More than a hundred people were injured. Two more are on life support. They may not survive the night."

Shepherd squeezed his eyes shut, feeling viscerally[5] the pain of loss of life, and at one of his events. He'd entered politics so he could help people. He'd never thought his events would be a place of death.

Carol went on, "Tampa Police were able to capture many of the perpetrators. They'll be held accountable for this tragedy."

"And what good does that do for the people killed? For their families?"

She didn't have an answer for that, sighing heavily as she dropped her head into her hands. Marcus Shepherd instead turned his attention to the TV, which was tuned into Fox news as it had been the entire evening, the anchors' voices low as they discussed the implications of that afternoon's attack. And that's what it was, pure and simple, a show of unprovoked violence aimed at hardworking Americans who didn't deserve to experience such terror. The anchors were picking apart the statement put out by the Democratic Socialists for American Freedom, which called Shepherd and his followers right-wing fascists[6], accusing them of fanning the flames of hatred. As if they weren't the ones who'd come to a peaceful rally armed and ready to kill. All the more reason he had to win again this November.

---

[5] Visceral – Coming from instinct rather than intellect, or to feel base, crude emotions.

[6] Fascist – One who believes in, supports, or sympathizes with an absolute dictator who uses force to suppress opposition and criticism, or a government system that promotes those same values

CHAPTER 2

EVERY TIME DAVID CHANDLER TURNED ON THE NEWS LATELY, he was more relieved than ever that he'd moved his family to the open countryside of Michigan's Upper Peninsula. Growing up in Detroit had taught him all too well how dangerous big cities could be. There were inconveniences to living miles from anyone else, sure, but that was a fair trade off to know his wife and kids were safe.

Three and a half years ago, he'd been hopeful about the future of his country. The people had come together under President Trump's leadership to weather the Coronavirus crisis; there'd been a renewed sense of community, a re-focusing on faith and family values, and for a moment it had seemed they were healing from the division and media-fueled hatred that had plagued the nation for most of his adult life. Unfortunately, it hadn't taken long for most of the people to forget the tough lessons learned during the pandemic. Soon enough, the liberal states out west were back to infringing on the rights of their people. David was afraid of what would happen if the democrats won the presidency in November, encouraging the spread of the anti-religion, anti-gun propaganda into the rest of the country.

Today's news coverage focused on the assault rifle ban recently passed in California, as it had nearly every day since the law passed the previous November. The state's governor, Emmanuel Santos, had insisted at first the buy-back and surrender program would be voluntary, but he'd known it would only be a matter of time before citizens' second amendment rights were violated under the guise of public safety. And now that time had come; the anchors cut away to live footage of a standoff in progress in Shasta County, which they described as a conservative Christian hold-out against the liberal politics common elsewhere in California. The footage was taken from above by a news helicopter and showed a SWAT team surrounding what looked like a farmhouse. Its inhabitant was barricaded inside, invisible to the camera's eye. A picture of came up on the upper right corner of the screen, showing a bearded, middle-aged man with his arm around a smiling woman in a floral dress, two boys in suits grinning in front of them. Change one of those boys to a girl, and it could be David's family on their way to Easter service. He seemed more like a normal guy than some kind of criminal. David wondered if the wife and kids were inside the house, too. How terrified must they be, to see all those men in riot gear swarming their front yard? David couldn't help noticing several of the SWAT members were carrying rifles far more powerful than those owned by the man they were threatening. Like they didn't even realize the whole point of the second amendment was to prevent the government from having this much more firepower than its people.

"What's going on, dad?" David's son, Joseph, said from the doorway. David considered changing the channel; Joe was only seven, and David would never let him watch movies or TV shows with this kind of violence. But this was real life, not a movie. As young as he was, he deserved to know the facts about what was happening in his country.

"The government is trying to take this man's guns away," David answered. "But the man doesn't want to give them up, so they're having a standoff. You don't have to worry, though. It's far away, in California."

Joe stepped further into the living room, stopping beside David's armchair with his eyes glued on the screen. "Can I watch with you?" he asked.

"Sure, bud," David answered, patting his lap. "Why don't you hop on up?"

The sound of running water through the kitchen doorway cut off. David heard the clink of the last plates from dinner being placed in the drying rack. A moment later, his wife, Marilyn, came into the room and sat down on the couch, their daughter Lillian right behind her. Lil was a couple years older than Joe; David felt less conflicted about her seeing the violent scene. They sat quietly while the Fox anchors explained the timeline of events so far, asking their reporter in the air about the mood of those on the scene.

"It seems a bit of overkill, doesn't it?" Lil asked. "An entire SWAT team for one guy with a gun?"

"They're probably hoping they'll scare him into coming out willingly," Marilyn answered.

David said, "Leave it to a Democrat governor to politicize fear rather than working with his citizens."

"It's understandable," Marilyn said. When she saw David's surprised look, she added, "Not that I agree with what they're doing. Just I get where the fear's coming from, after that last mass shooting in LA. More than a hundred dead in ten minutes. That has to be the worst one we've seen yet. Of course people would want to do something to prevent it happening again."

David said, "That's the excuse they're using. How many people own guns in this country? Just because one of them happened to be a deranged madman doesn't mean the rest of us are a threat. That's as ridiculous as banning cars just because one idiot drives drunk."

Marilyn said, "You're right, but that's using logic. People do some stupid things when they're afraid."

David couldn't argue with that. The family watched in silence until the live coverage cut back to the anchors' faces. They praised the man's commitment to his rights, saying a prayer that the incident would end without bloodshed. David couldn't help but wonder what stations like CNN were reporting on the topic. Likely they were praising the ban and the SWAT team action. He wondered if CNN viewers had seen the same picture of the man Fox showed. He would guess not; more likely they'd found one where he was dressed in camo, maybe posing with his guns, or crouched beside a buck he'd bagged during hunting season.

The news anchors shifted topics with a promise they'd return to the scene of the stand-off if there were any developments. They began discussing the recent stock market dip and David turned down the volume, telling his family, "There's something I wanted to tell you all, now that we're all here. Something I didn't want to bring up over dinner."

Marilyn looked alarmed as she asked, "Is everything alright?"

"Completely," David said. "It's more about the future than the present. You know that old army airfield up by the Hiawatha Forest?"

"The abandoned one we visited a few years ago?" Marilyn asked.

"That's the one," David answered. "Well there are a couple underground missile silos on the site. Completely abandoned, not being used for anything anymore. Today I bought one."

"We own a missile silo?" Joe asked from his lap, eyes wide with excitement.

"You did what?" Marilyn asked on his heels, no small amount of accusation in her eyes; normally they would have talked about any purchase of that size, and David did feel a bit guilty about not running it by her first. She wouldn't have seen the necessity for it, though. It was one of those times he figured it was better to ask forgiveness than permission, as Martin Luther would have said. Marilyn asked, "Just what possible reason could we have to own a missile silo?"

David explained, "There's plenty of room inside for all four of us—more room than there is in our house, honestly. We could bring the neighbors along if we wanted to. And it's built to withstand just about anything. If things start to get worse after the election in November, I want us to have a place we can go. I'll get it stocked up in the next couple months, make sure there's plenty of food and water, fuel for the generators, all of that kind of stuff."

Lil's eyes went wider the longer he talked. She said, "You think there's gonna be a war, Daddy? Is the world gonna end?"

"Well, Sweetheart, I hope not. But if something bad happens, won't you feel better knowing we'll be able to survive it? Be prepared. That's what they teach you in Boy Scouts, isn't it champ?" David said this last with a playful jab at Joe's shoulder. Even though his son hadn't said anything, David could see from his eyes he was just as worried as his sister. And Marilyn—she was still glaring daggers at him from the couch. She'd be mad for a couple days, probably, especially once she found out just how much David had spent on the silo. Let her be upset. He hoped she was right, honestly, that it ended up being a frivolous purchase, that they'd never use it and he'd be stuck spending his retirement eating canned meat and army field rations. Deep down, though, he had a feeling she'd be thanking him for the foresight sooner rather than later. That feeling only intensified as the news cut back to the stand-off in California, the SWAT team moving in toward the farmhouse, the first flashes of fire spitting from their rifles.

CHAPTER 3

AFTER TWELVE YEARS AS A SENATOR, Marcus Shepherd knew a thing or two about how the typical campaign season went. With roughly nine months to go before the election in November, his schedule should be busy with rallies and appearances. Talking to his supporters had always been one of his favorite parts about being a politician. It was why he'd gotten into politics to begin with: to help those who were oppressed, returning justice and balance to a long-corrupted system. But after the attack in Florida in January—just a month ago, though it felt much longer—there had been a rash of copy-cat attacks at other right-wing events around the country, and even more threats from ANTIFA groups and other radical organizations. There'd been no more fatalities, thank God, but his campaign managers and security had deemed the risk too great. All his rallies had been cancelled, replaced by virtual fireside chats held in secure locations. Exactly the kind of restriction of freedoms he was working so hard to combat.

By his original campaign schedule, Shepherd should have been in his home state of Ohio this week. Today would have been a fundraising event at the Great Columbus Convention Center. He would have just arrived that morning after a rally in Cincinnati; after that, there had been scheduled stops at factories in Toledo and Cleveland to talk to the workers and hear their concerns, ending his tour of the state at the Wright Patterson Air Force Base in Dayton. Instead, he was hunkered down in his Capitol Hill office, preparing to deliver a televised speech to his followers. He'd tried to make the most of the unfortunate situation, reading some of the bills that would soon be voted on in the senate with his surplus of time, but his frustration was making it difficult to focus on such mundanities. What use was it to review congressional budgets when his people were being subjected to such violence? This wasn't the America he'd grown up loving, and he was more afraid for the future of his nation than he wanted to admit.

But today was no time to give in to those fears. The most important thing a president could do, in his estimation, was to lead with strength, by example. Maybe he couldn't speak to the workers face-to-face, but he could still speak to their hearts—and, more crucial still, let them know someone in Washington could hear them. Shepherd watched the film crew bustling around the office. The lights were set, the microphones in place, the cameras on and ready to broadcast. There was a minute of sudden silence as the sound technicians took their levels, and when they nodded, satisfied, Shepherd checked his watch. Seven on the dot; he imagined the anchors on the stations broadcasting his speech killing time, reviewing his anticipated talking points. Waiting for his signal.

"Are we all set?" Shepherd asked the cameraman.

"Ready when you are, Sir," he answered.

"Excellent," Shepherd said, folding his hands atop his desk. "Let's not keep America waiting."

With that he smiled into the camera as the crew gave him the final countdown.

Emmanuel Santos was reviewing the security reports at his office in Los Angeles when Mehar Ali entered in her usual quiet way, standing patiently in front of his desk until he looked up to acknowledge her. The reports today were no different than they'd been for the last month. Three more suspicious packages had been pulled out of his incoming mail that morning; two had contained white powder, likely to be revealed as anthrax once the lab reports came back. It made it seem all the more pointless that his staffers had insisted he cancel his in-person events for the month. Not much point isolating him from the public, he thought; it just made the right-wing radicals bring their violence to his doorstep.

Santos rubbed his eyes wearily, set the reports aside, and looked up to acknowledge Mehar.

"Senator Shepherd is beginning his talk, sir," they said. "Would you like to watch it?"

"Not particularly," Santos answered, giving them a smile to soften the response. "I'm more interested in what my democratic challengers are up to. How are we looking for Super Tuesday?"

Mehar answered, "You're polling six points ahead of Senator Ocasio-Cortez. Andrew Yang and Governor Martin are the only ones close behind her."

Santos nodded. Those were good numbers, but he knew better than to take them completely at face value. Still, he was in good shape to get the nomination. He'd won Iowa and Nevada by a fair margin, came in a close second in New Hampshire. He expected he would lose South Carolina on Friday, but if those poll numbers turned out correct he'd make up any lost ground in the delegate count when the votes were tallied after Super Tuesday. And not much he could do about any of it now, in either case.

Santos asked, "Is CNN broadcasting Shepherd's talk?"

"No, sir."

"Good. Put it on, would you?"

Mehar smirked as she crossed the office and turned on the TV.

Two hundred miles north, in Redding, California, Nate Wilson pulled the hood of his sweatshirt down lower over his face as he hurried down Market Street. He was later than he'd meant to be, had no doubt already missed half of Marcus Shepherd's address. But Nate didn't need to hear everything the man said, he reassured himself. He already knew Shepherd's platform in depth, felt it in his heart; he'd never been a fan of lifetime politicians, on either side, but if anyone had to run the country Shepherd was the best man for the job.

Nate veered off the main road just past the long-abandoned Redding Inn, dipping through the hole in the fence around it to take a shortcut through the weed-ravaged parking lot. Just one more small business that had been decimated by the unfair policies put in place by his state's liberal lawmakers. Shasta County was full of them. As if he needed more fuel for the fire of revolution that had burned in him these past eight years. His destination was on the other side of the crumbling tan-and-brown inn, a nondescript building that, for most people, didn't warrant a second thought or look. Anyone looking at it from the outside probably assumed it was just one more abandoned warehouse, another decrepit monument to their crumbling economy. And that was exactly how Nate and his compatriots wanted it. The perfect cover for the work toward liberation that went on within.

At the door, Nate knocked twice, paused, then knocked twice more, the secret code that would rouse whoever was manning the door within. The slit in the metal door opened, Matt Horner's wide blue eyes peering through then crinkling at the edges in a smile when he saw it was Nate.

"You're late," Matt said.

"Got held up at work," Nate explained. "Had an F150 with a bad tranny get brought in last minute."

Matt's face withdrew from the door slit and Nate heard the clunk of the four locks being undone. A moment later, the heavy door creaked open just enough for him to slide through. He asked Matt, "Everyone else in the basement?"

"Yessir," Matt answered. "Think they're just watching Shepherd talk now, though. Don't think you missed anything important."

Nate clasped the young man's shoulder and muttered thanks, then went down the dark hallway and found the door to the staircase. He heard Shepherd's deep, soothing voice booming out of the speakers as he began his descent, drowning out the overlapping chatter of those watching. Their group had been growing, these past couple years. The basement was large enough for them for now, but if they gained many more members they'd have to start looking for another space. A good problem to have, he figured. They could use as many hands as they could get. Nate entered to few greetings, most of the people gathered on the ratty couches and folding chairs that furnished the space too intent on the screen for distraction. Shepherd was speaking to the conditions in former car factories in Ohio, another state that had been gutted by unfair policies taking the jobs from hardworking citizens under the guise of environmental action. The liberals always put a fancy window dressing on their policies, like they thought that would keep people from seeing what they really were: a restriction of freedom, a shattering of the American dream. But the people saw through it, more and more with each passing day.

Nate took a seat beside Bill Shaffer, dressed in the camo-print vest and hunter orange hat that were his standard uniform, his AR-15 propped against his leg. Bill brought that thing out any chance he got, proud of having spared it from the state's buy-back program all those years ago. Bill was another original member of their militia, if anything more a driving force behind it, after his neighbor was killed in that stand-off at his farm the month the assault rifle ban was passed.

"How are we looking for next week?" Nate asked him.

"Good," Bill answered, distractedly, his eyes still glued on the TV screen against the wall. "We've gathered most of the armaments we need. Just need to track down a couple grenades, a few more bits of armor."

"How many we got on board for the Reckoning?" Nate asked.

Bill answered, "Seventeen. Should be plenty."

"And they'll never see us coming," Nate said, nodding his satisfaction. He'd long ago learned that the media was the biggest enemy of American freedom. Those talking heads were the ones putting fear in everybody's hearts, making them feel like they had to give up their rights for the sake of safety. But it had never been an either-or proposition, and on Tuesday they were going to take that message national. It was time the media learned they couldn't warp the narrative anymore. It was time to take their country back.

Marcus Shepherd finished his address, prompting a chorus of claps and cheers from the assembled militia members.

"Right," Bill said, "Time to get to work." He turned off the TV amidst a shuffling of chairs as they formed up in a circle, one of the others passing around copies of their mission details. Nate glanced over it with a smirk. It was shaping up to be a Super Tuesday, indeed.

CHAPTER 4

THE MEDIA HAD ALWAYS ANNOYED PAT JACOBS, but the older she got, the more useless it seemed to get. She was, admittedly, a bit of a curmudgeon[7]—she was only in her mid-thirties, but she'd been born an old soul, her mama had always said—but she didn't think it was just her perception. The media was increasingly divisive and obsessive, less concerned with the facts than it was with being outraged. And on both sides; even her one-time go-tos like Fox and Breitbart were annoying her of late, and she wasn't the only one who said so. Six months after the assault rifle ban passed in California, it still seemed to be the main thing any news outlet wanted to talk about, undeterred by the fact there'd been nothing new to say on the topic since the last armed stand-off in mid-March. The big talk now was that similar legislation had passed a few weeks back in Oregon and Washington, as if that were a surprise to anyone; they always played copycat to California's legislation, like annoying little siblings desperate for approval. Still, no point to harp on it to citizens of Nevada. That kind of restrictive legislation would never fly here. One of the reasons she'd bought one of the decommissioned silos of Area 25 as the home for her off the grid community.

Pat was accustomed to not fitting into any of the pre-determined political boxes in her country. She'd been a registered Libertarian since she'd

---

[7] Curmudgeon – A difficult or argumentative person

voted for Gary Johnson back in 2012 but even that had been a compromise. She didn't appreciate the hypocritical moralizing of Republicans any more than she liked Democrats dictating what she could own and say, and she'd yet to see a politician that spent her tax money the way she thought they should. The truth was, there was no party that fit a Christian feminist who believed the best thing a government could do for its citizens was stay out of their way.

Pat switched her truck's radio from AM to FM. Even the limited selections available on the dial in the sparsely-populated deserts of central Nevada were an improvement over the political talking heads, right now; at least the music she could tune out. She settled on a station playing upbeat selections in Spanish as she navigated her pickup off 95 and onto the surface roads of Beatty.

There wasn't much in Beatty, Nevada, just a smattering of gas stations, hotels, and stores clustered around the 95/374 junction, but that was one of the things Pat liked about the little town. They had most everything she needed for her bi-weekly restocking trip—save the times she needed a feed store for the livestock, when she'd instead make the drive south to Pahrump—and she didn't have to deal with the rampant tourists and consumerism of Las Vegas and its surrounding area. The longer she lived out in the desert, surrounded only by like-minded off-the-gridders, the more jarring it was to re-enter so-called normal society. She'd tried sending others out for supplies for a while, but they inevitably forgot something important and she'd soon realized it was better to just make the trip herself. Pat parked her truck in the furthest row of the lot, like she always did; she didn't mind pushing her cart a bit further, and there was less chance out here someone would ding her door or take pictures of the seemingly-contradicting bumper stickers covering the tailgate. Another advantage of the small towns over Vegas. She'd gotten into her fair share of arguments with random citizens in Vegas, who took her bumper stickers as an invitation to debate rather than what they were: a free-speech declaration of her ideals.

If there was one think Pat Jacobs hated more than self-important politicians, it was needless drama.

As she turned toward the grocery store, though, Pat realized she wasn't going to be able to avoid drama here. A small crowd was gathered around the front doors of the store, protesting something or another. From the placards in their hands, it could've been anything from the minimum wage to health care to the price of milk; these protest groups were always bad at keeping on-message. There weren't more than two-dozen people walking around outside, but of course there were plenty of news vans there to cover the scene anyway. No doubt they'd blow it up into some big stink in the broadcasts, using their usual misleading camera angles, interviewing only the angriest among them.

If she were in a different mood, Pat would've lowered her head and pushed right on through, but today she just didn't have the patience. She spun on her heel and climbed back into her cab, bringing the same trumpet-heavy song back to life on the radio. She stabbed at the power button, silencing it, as she pulled out of the parking lot and headed toward the dollar store down the street. Their selection wasn't as good, but at least their prices were right. As she drove, she thought—not for the first time—that it was past time for her community to start making their own flour and butter. Make themselves truly self-sufficient. It would be hard work, sure, but worth it to never have to interact with idiots.

The sun was just starting to set as Nate Wilson pulled into the parking lot of the Redding Inn, his beat-up '04 Wrangler sputtering like it might die before he put the thing in park. Only in America would a car mechanic drive a beater because he couldn't afford new parts, he thought to himself bitterly. Hopefully, Earl was behind the desk at the inn, would let him do some maintenance work in exchange for a room again. Nate's credit cards were all maxed out, his bank account balance hovering dangerously close to zero, and the few dollars in his pocket wouldn't be enough for a night, not even at a run-down motel like the Redding Inn. He sat behind the wheel a moment after he killed the engine, lamenting his bad luck as the wind whipped the garbage bag he'd hastily taped up over the missing side window of the soft top. Usually he just left it open, but he'd piled all his worldly possessions back there before leaving the house. The last thing he needed today was for his stuff to get ruined if it decided to rain.

Sheila had kicked Nate out before, but never like this. There was no yelling this time, just a weary, cold indifference, a noncommittal suggestion he could swing by to see the kids, maybe, next week sometime, the vagueness of the date indicating said visit would never happen. And on Nate's birthday, no less. Turning 27 today and his life was no better than it had been when he was 18. Worse even. Homeless, under-employed, with two kids he'd have to fight just to spend time with. The liberals talking about white privilege would bite their tongues if they saw his life.

Nate opened the door to his Jeep with a heavy sigh, the oppressively hot air hitting him in the face as he let the last of the AC out into the world. A man dressed in camo vest and seed cap was leaning against the wall by the motel office entrance, a half-smoked cigarette dangling from his right hand. Nate made to move past him but the man tracked him with his gaze, and when Nate was close enough said, "Nice Jeep."

Nate couldn't tell if he was being sarcastic; he gave a noncommittal nod in return, said, "It's just an old junker."

The man shrugged, said, "Wrangler's a classic, though. Even if it's seen better days. Just like it's owner, I gather."

Nate said, "Yeah, well. Been a hell of a day." Hell of a life, was more like it.

The man in the camo vest chuckled without humor. "Lots of people feeling that way these days. Stuck in the mud, and no roots around to pull themselves out."

"Ain't that the truth," Nate answered.

"Doesn't have to be that way, though," the man said. He took a long pull from his cigarette, blowing the smoke up at the sky, and said, "Matter of fact, me and some like-minded folk are about to meet up, talk about ways we can turn things around."

"That so?" Nate asked.

"Mm-hmm," the man answered. "And you know, you seem like you'd fit right in to our crew. That is, if you're not busy tonight."

Nate looked from the man to the Redding Inn office, considering. He certainly didn't have anything better on his agenda, even if he felt a bit wary of heading off with a strange man encountered in a motel parking lot. That was how horror movies started, a voice said from the back of his mind.

"Wish I could," Nate answered, finally. "But I've gotta get myself some place to stay tonight. Probably gonna have to work off the rate, too. If they'll let me."

"Old lady kick you out?" the man asked.

"How'd you guess?"

"I know that look," he said. "Worn it a few times myself. If you're hurting, I've got an extra room since my little girl went off to college."

Nate asked, "If I join your group, you mean?"

The man tossed his cigarette butt down, grounding it out under his boot. "No catches, no strings. Just one man helping out another. I'll even throw in a few beers. You look like you could use 'em."

Nate looked the man up and down. He seemed normal enough. Probably a hunter, something he could respect; he used to go out for every season, back when he could still afford his yearly license. And anyway, what did he have to lose? Even counting the Wrangler, his belongings couldn't have been worth more than a grand. Hell, even if the guy killed him, he might be doing Nate a favor, at this point.

"I sure appreciate it," Nate said. "And I'd like to meet your friends, anyway. I'm just about sick of letting life push me around."

The man held out his hand and said, "Name's Bill Shaffer."

"Nate Wilson," Nate answered, shaking the offered hand, appreciative of Bill's firm grip; that was a real man's handshake, right there.

"Well come on," Bill said, starting for the stairs to lead them to the motel's second floor of doors. "Meeting starts right at six, and Fred always kicks things off passing around a jar of his homemade moonshine. Don't want to miss that."

Bill said this with a wink over his shoulder as he mounted the steps, and the last of Nate's trepidation[8] faded. He liked this Bill, he decided. Maybe his luck was finally starting to turn around.

---

[8] Trepidation – wariness, fear, or alarm

CHAPTER 5

Super Tuesday, 6:30PM California time. The polls in eastern states like Massachusetts and Vermont had been closed long enough and the states were starting to report initial Democratic primary results—the only primary reporters and viewers of CNN's Los Angeles studio cared about; an unexpected early lead from Andrew Yang in North Carolina gave the anchors plenty to talk about while they waited for the west coast's polls to close. Closed off inside the studio, the anchors couldn't see the sun setting over the city outside, sending long shadows stretching from the massive buildings of the LA skyline. Even if there had been windows in the studio, they wouldn't have shown the seventeen figures slinking through those shadows toward the rear door of the studio. All seventeen had dressed carefully for the Reckoning. Even if they were spotted, there was nothing suspicious about their dark jackets and blue jeans. Their guns were carefully concealed in gym bags or waist bands, their masks tucked into their pockets; they planned to wait for the right time to show their true intentions.

The two security guards keeping watch over the back door of the studio scanned the alley it faced with their usual bored half-attention. Between them, they had more than fifteen years of experience, mostly guarding this very door, and in those fifteen years neither had been given cause to draw his service pistol or dealt with anything more dangerous than a few angry protesters.

The crime in Los Angeles rarely made it to the kind of neighborhood where the studio was built. Its employees were insulated from those violent realities.

At least, they had been until today. The seventeen figures lined up between two buildings across the alley from the studio's back door. Nate poked his head out for a quick look; neither security guard seemed to have moved since the last time he looked.

"What's the time?" Bill asked behind him.

"Six forty," Matt answered. "Think we should go?"

Nate and Bill shared a look. Their goal was to take the air right at seven, figuring it to be when the most viewers would be turned in, when they'd have the best chance of having their message be widely heard. It seemed a bit early to him, still. But then, they weren't sure what obstacles they'd meet on their way in to the studio. There would be three more security guards to subdue inside, according to the scouting reports they'd done the last week, and plenty of civilians, from sound techs to make-up people to janitors. No telling if any of them would decide to be a hero.

"Alright," Nate said, with a decisive nod. "Let's move."

Nate and Bill stepped out into the alley and walked toward the studio back door, doing their best to look casual—lost tourists, was the vibe they'd decided to go with. They were nearly within striking distance of the guards before they even looked up, the older of the two shouting, "Hey, buddies, this is private property. You can't be back here."

"Could you maybe give us some directions?" Bill asked in reply; his slight drawl, they decided, made him a better choice for playing the role of clueless country boy. "See, we were trying to get to the Universal tour, but I think we took a wrong turn…"

Both guards focused on Bill as he walked up, holding out his phone. With their attention distracted, Nate came up behind the younger guard and whipped out the move he'd been practicing for weeks, pulling the man's pistol from his holster and tossing it aside with one hand while he locked his other elbow around the guard's neck into a chokehold. Bill moved fast for an old man. He had the second guard on the ground before he could react, pinning him there with a knee in his back.

"Take off your radios and toss 'em," Bill ordered. The guards obeyed. The rest of their militia poured out into the alley once they saw the guards were secured. In short order, they had both bound and gagged. Nate slid the keys off of the older one's belt.

"That's step one done," Bill said. "Everybody get to your positions. You know what to do."

Nate took a second to appreciate their militia's efficiency. They'd practiced what they'd do over and over back at their headquarters in Redding, had studied the studio blueprints until they were seared into Nate's brain. Once the back door was open they paused just long enough to pull out their guns and don their masks, then Bill led six of their members straight through, bound for the main entrance. They'd neutralize the two guards there, hold the door, cut the phone lines. The police would show up eventually, of course, but if they did this right they'd have enough time to read their full grievances before the law arrived. Two of them would stay at the back door, keeping watch over the guards and the entrance; the rest of them would follow Nate up to the studio, where the anchors were no doubt still talking through their points, completely unaware of the chaos about to descend on them.

"Stay alert," Nate whispered to his crew as they climbed the cement stairs of the fire exit. The last guard should be at the door to the studio, but he did rounds periodically, on a schedule they hadn't been able to determine. At the top of the staircase they exited out into a long hallway, lined the whole way down by dressing rooms. All the doors were shut; Nate passed them warily, ears straining for the sound of a turning latch or creaking hinge. He heard a muffled cough, turned his head to look back, but if it was someone in one of the rooms they weren't making themselves known.

"Look out!" Matt shouted suddenly behind him, and Nate turned, saw the fifth roving security guard coming into view around the corner. Matt had his rifle raised, pulled the trigger before Nate could stop him. The guard fell to the ground. Nate muttered a curse and rushed forward to him. Commotion down the hall said there had been plenty of people behind those doors, people who were now peeking their heads out, curious at first though that quickly shifted to panic when they saw the armed militia standing there, guns drawn, faces covered.

"Secure them!" Nate ordered as he reached the guard. The man was whimpering, in pain, but still alive; the bullet had grazed off his shoulder. He'd need stitches, but he'd live.

"I told you not to fire unless you had to," Nate said to Matt, who'd followed him toward the guard. "If we kill people, that's all people will remember."

Matt replied, "I'm sorry. I panicked."

Nate shook his head. Matt was younger than the rest of them, and he'd been afraid of something like this, but Bill had insisted the boy was ready for real action. But no irreparable damage done, Nate told himself, as he turned his attention down the hallway. The rest of the militia was rounding up the people from the dressing rooms. Thankfully, no one was resisting; in short order, all of them were bound and locked back in one of the rooms.

"You stay here with the guard," Nate ordered Matt. "Keep pressure on the wound. And keep an eye on that room of hostages. Got it?"

Matt's hands were shaking as he pressed his hands down on the guard's shoulder, but he nodded and complied. They had a schedule to keep; Nate had to just hope he would keep things in hand here. At least the guard was neutralized, Nate told himself as his group continued on their way, finally reaching the studio doors without any further incidents. He checked the time on his phone: 6:55. Almost perfect.

U all set? he texted to Bill.

A moment later, Bill replied, *All secure. One guard resisted, had to break his arm. Everyone else came peacefully.*

The best news Nate could hope for. It was time to carry out their Reckoning.

The camera crew were the first ones to react when the militia burst through the studio doors. A few tried to rush at them but quickly stopped, arms rising in the air once they saw the rifles in everyone's hands. Someone screamed; the voices on the stage hesitated, stopped, the anchors peering into the shadows beyond their stage lights.

"This is a takeover!" Nate announced, storming the stage, pointing his gun toward the man cameraman and ordering him, "Keep that rolling! I've got a message to deliver."

The militia stormed the stage. The male anchor stood up. "You can't just storm in here like this. This is a closed—"

He was silenced by the crack of a rifle butt hitting the side of his face and collapsed in a heap behind the news desk. Another militia member pulled the female anchor from the other seat, dragging her out of the camera's view, clearing the way for Nate to step up. He mounted the stage with unhurried steps, projecting an air of confidence. Once there, he waited for the sounds of the takeover around him to fade to quiet moans and sobs. Then he began.

"I'm here today on behalf of the American people," he said into the camera, delivering the speech he'd practiced dozens of times the past week, maybe even hundreds, until he could recite it word for word. "Of all the American people, not just the rich and powerful, the liberal elites. The Americans who work hard and don't have enough to show for it. The ones who are the real backbone of this country. And we're fed up with being ignored. The liberal media doesn't have any interest in giving voice to our concerns. They're too busy making a comfortable little bubble for their viewers, too busy putting their spin on the facts and turning it into fake news to turn the people against each other.

"But this ends today. We, the people, are America, and we are done letting the government trample on our rights. Too many of the people in power act like they've never heard of the Bill of Rights, like they can violate the constitution without any consequences. I'm here to tell you that this is your consequence. We are done working ourselves to death so the rich can get richer and find new ways to hold us down. We will no longer stand for having our guns taken away, the ones the Second Amendment guarantees us the right to carry. Neither will we stand for the religious oppression against Christians. No law can be made that prevents people practicing their religion. That's what the First Amendment says, just before it says we, the people, have the right to assemble and make the government hear our complaints.

"So consider this our redress of grievances. We will hold this television station until we're forcibly removed. Peaceful protest has gotten us nowhere. It seems like the only thing people pay attention to in this country is violence. We're not here to hurt anybody if we can help it. But we can't keep standing by, silent, while our rights are trampled and our lives are destroyed. The time has come to take our country back and put the power back into the hands of our citizens, where it was when this great nation was founded. Where it should have been all along. And if you agree with me, if you're tired of being pushed aside and told what you're allowed to do, how you're allowed to live—well, then, I'm calling on you to stand up, too. Push back. Show your congressmen and senators, your so-called representatives, where the real power lies. Show the media they can't feed you lies anymore. We all deserve better. If we come together we can right these wrongs and turn America into the country it should have been all along."

Nate felt his phone shake, glanced at the screen. There was a text there from Bill. *Hear sirens coming*, the text said, *police are incoming*. But that was fine, Nate thought to himself. Let them come; he'd said his piece, and said it live. There was nothing they could do now to stop what he'd set in motion.

CHAPTER 6

BLAKE DAVIS HAD NEVER BELIEVED VIOLENCE WAS THE ANSWER. He'd remained a committed pacifist even as he watched fascists and white supremacists gain a foothold in his country, threatening and murdering their way through minority communities. He had seen it as a point of strength for those who shared his beliefs. They would not stoop to the level of the aggressors; they were better that that, would rise through compassion and peace, not anger and division. When California had passed its assault rifle ban two years ago, he'd genuinely believed these anti-violence values were gaining traction. Finally there had been a real change in policy, an acknowledgment of the fact that the Second Amendment had been written in a different time, when a single man with a single gun couldn't cause hundreds of casualties in an hour. Other states had followed California's lead, enacting their own bans, including Blake's home-state of Oregon, and he'd watched this news he'd started to feel a cautious hope. Maybe things really could change. The little people really could shift the path of policy; the government wasn't the massive, immovable machine he'd feared.

Then the protests started. The stand-offs. Blake watched in growing horror as armed militias formed on both coasts and the heartlands in between. He couldn't stop himself from tallying the dead. It was one thing for these protestors to kill the police sent to enforce the gun buy-backs—

cops and soldiers had at least signed up to put themselves in harm's way, and anyway he didn't completely agree with their tactics in the best of times—but each innocent bystander who died cut him to the core. Many nights, he found himself awake until dawn, scrolling through the hateful speech these right-wing radicals spewed all over the internet. If he could see their point of view, maybe he could understand. But all it did was make him angrier. Surer there would be no bridging the widening gap between the opposing factions that were tearing his country apart.

There'd been pushback from the eastern half of Oregon since the state's assault rifle ban went into effect, but it had come to a head in the general election two weeks before. Republican politician Samuel Evans had been building a quiet following as mayor of Bend and used the right-wing anger over the ban to catapult himself into a bid for the state legislature. No one in Blake's liberal echo chamber in Eugene thought he had a realistic chance of winning—not until election night, when the votes, while close, came down in favor of Evans. The incumbent whose seat he took had been one of the strongest advocates of the new gun legislation, a source of hope for Blake and those who shared his ideals, proof positive that good people could fight back against violent tyranny.

It was on election night that Blake Davis realized pacifism had no place in the current political climate. During his victory speech, Samuel Evans had announced his plans to overturn the assault rifle ban, prompting loud cheers from his crowd of followers, many of whom were openly carrying their weapons, proud of living in violation of state laws. Those same followers were the ones who'd show up to black lives matter protests with blue lives matter signs. The hypocrisy of them supporting the side that had resulted in so many police deaths over the past two years was more than Blake could wrap his head around.

And Blake wasn't the only one who felt this way, he soon realized. A friend who was a member of an anti-fascist activist group invited him to a meeting to plan radical action. He found himself nodding along as the group's leader said from the podium, "The fascists in this country don't have room in their minds for rational debate. We can talk at them all they want, but they're never going to listen. The only language they understand is violence, and it's past time for us to start sending a message they'll understand."

Which was how, a little more than two weeks later, Blake Davis found himself standing with a dozen like-minded fellow anti-fascist organizers outside Samuel Evans' congressional campaign office in Bend, Oregon, armed with a can of spray paint in each hand and a bag of bricks and rocks weighing heavily on his shoulder. It was early evening, the sun just set and the sky above a darkening gray. Through the plate glass windows of the office he saw half a dozen staffers milling about, chatting, working. No sign of Senator Evans himself, which was a shame; ideally, in Blake's mind, he was the one who had something to answer for.

"I won't lie to you," their leader said in his final pep talk, looking over their masked faces. "Some of us will be arrested. Some of us might be hurt, or killed. But no injustice was ever solved by good people sitting by and letting evil run rampant. The sacrifices we all make today will not be in vain!"

Their responding cheers were loud enough some of the workers inside the congressional office glanced up, peering through the plate glass. But it was dark enough outside Blake doubted they could see much. They probably assumed it was just another protest; there'd been one here nearly every day since the senator's election. The young man whose desk was closest to the window was the only one still looking when Blake stopped on the sidewalk and hurled the first brick. The massive window shattered, glass fragments raining down on those inside.

From there, the world descended into chaos. Everything was screams and shouts—terror from the inside, anger from those there to vandalize. About half of their group stepped through the new holes where the windows had been, swinging bats into computers, ripping posters from the walls. Blake stopped outside, instead, using his spray paint to emblazon a massive anarchist A in red over the front door. Others were writing slogans on the walls, inside and out: *You can silence a gun but you can't silence people; Stop enabling murder; Our blood is on your hands.* Blake smelled smoke, looked around. Their group's leader had shoved a piece of cloth into the neck of a liquor bottle and now held a lighter to the trailing end of the accelerant-soaked wick. A Molotov cocktail, Blake realized in the second before he threw it back toward the rear offices, the explosion generating flames that licked along the walls. Blake tried not to think about whether there were people back there. Whether there were exits. Whether they were murderers.

Blake entered the office, then, holding an arm up over his eyes against the black smoke, one of the staffers was huddled in the corner, on her cellphone. Calling the police. One of the protestors—Blake couldn't tell who, with their faces covered—pulled her up roughly, smacking the phone out of her hand and crushing it under the heel of his boot. Which seemed like a pointless gesture, Blake thought. All the noise they were making, the police would be here any moment; he was a bit surprised he wasn't hearing sirens already. The woman sobbed, terrified, as the protestor smacked her across the face, hard enough she fell onto the scattered glass shards on the ground. She laid there, completely still; he couldn't tell whether she was unconscious or had simply given up, resigned to the violence erupting around her. Blake felt a brief pang of regret as he stared down at her limp form. But it wasn't his fault, Blake insisted in his own head. He wanted to be a pacifist, had always been a pacifist. People like her—they were the ones who'd forced him into this. They deserved to suffer, he told himself, as he reached into his bag and retrieved another brick.

CHAPTER 7

WATCHING THE ATTACK ON THE TV STATION IN LOS ANGELES
the previous March had chilled Emmanuel Santos to the bone. It had been
a sheer miracle nobody had been killed, the way that armed militia stormed
the place, waving their guns around. Illegal guns, Santos hadn't been able
to help himself from noting, though that was among the least of the offenses
those who'd been caught were charged with. By this point, fifteen militia
members had been arrested and sat awaiting trial in a maximum security
prison, one Santos doubted most of them would be out of for decades, given
the extent of their charges. Only a minor relief, he was sure, for those who'd
been injured in the attack.

As much as it had pained and angered him to see the violence, though,
he couldn't deny the attack had also proven helpful to his campaign. It had
proved the need for the legislation he'd introduced banning assault rifles
in California six years ago, something his supporters had been quick to
point out. The rise in violence had affected his competitors in the Democratic primary, as well, giving them another reason to drop out of the race
once the Super Tuesday results showed Santos had a substantial lead in the
delegate count. By the end of that week, the race had been reduced only to
him and Senator Ocasio-Cortez, and even she had suspended her run, citing
the need for the party to unite against their common enemy as other conservative militias across the country launched similar attacks in the weeks
that followed. Since mid-April, Santos had been able to shift his focus ex-

clusively to his opponent across the aisle. He'd had months to study Marcus Shepherd's policies and voting record, to dig into the less favorable aspects of his personal life—his failed first marriage, the gay brother he'd disowned, the fact that his children shared almost none of his political beliefs. All those details had provided excellent material for a series of television ads questioning the man's integrity, though to be honest Santos was more concerned with Shepherd's politics. Today, in their first debate, those politics were where he planned to focus his attention.

Emmanuel Santos had been looking forward to this debate. He knew all too well his previous speeches and events had been mostly preaching to the choir, as it were. With how polarized the nation's media had become, he highly doubted anyone paid attention to them that didn't already plan to vote for him in November. This debate, though, would be seen by voters from both parties. His first chance to share his opinions with those who didn't share his views. It was unlikely he'd bring any Republican voters to his side, but he liked to imagine not everyone who identified on the right believed in environmental destruction and economic policies that favored the rich, and those were two of the cornerstones of Shepherd's campaign.

As he watched his own eyes in the mirror of his dressing room, Santos ran through his opening remarks. He'd rehearsed them time and time again, knew the words forward and backward, but proper preparation prevented poor performance, as his father had always told him. He was determined to make the strongest possible showing on that stage. He heard the door open behind him, saw Mehar Ali's reflection appear behind him in the mirror.

"Are they ready for me?" Santos asked his campaign manager.

"They want you on the stage in five," she answered, smiling in her reassuring way as she asked, "What about you? Are you ready?"

"More than you know," Santos answered. He tightened the knot of his tie, flashing his teeth at the mirror, and stood. It was time to take his platform to the people. All the people.

"Debate's about to start, kids!" David Chandler shouted into the kitchen as the Fox News anchors on the TV screen cut away to the moderator for his opening remarks.

"Coming, Dad!" Lillian shouted back. A second later, both her and Joseph entered through the kitchen doorway, their mother close behind them. Each of them had a bowl of ice cream; Marilyn was carrying two, passing one to David as she settled down on the couch. She'd made him an impressive-looking sundae, complete with whipped cream and a cherry on top. It was a fitting dessert for what he was sure would be an entertaining evening. Based on what he heard on the news, David fully expected Shepherd would easily come out on top at the end of the day.

Emmanuel Santos was the first to speak tonight. David focused on his ice cream, mostly tuning out his voice, which was rehashing the same left-wing talking points he'd heard from Democrats the past decade or more. It wasn't until he heard Marcus Shepherd's voice cut in that David looked up, wondering if he'd missed the start of the Senator's remarks. But no; the cameras were scrambling to shift their focus, not expecting Shepherd to interject, "…can't just let you spread lies so blatantly without trying to make you see reality. Those militia members aren't terrorists, they're fighting for the freedoms your party—"

"You'll have your chance to talk, Mr. Shepherd," the moderator interrupted. "Mr. Santos, if you'd continue?"

David met his wife's gaze over their kids' heads. It seemed tonight's debate was about to get particularly interesting.

Barely twenty minutes in and this was already the most exciting debate Pat Jacobs had ever watched. She'd mostly put it on to have something in the background while she prepared the week's batch of bread for the community, but with Shepherd and Santos interrupting each other and tossing insults back and forth, it was turning out to be some unexpectedly entertaining television.

The two candidates calmed a bit during the first round of questions, which focused mostly on the differences in their environmental policies—a hot-button issue for the left, and one Pat cared about, too, but not much of a debate point; Shepherd's campaign was built around social issues more than those kinds of policies. Pat focused on punching down the risen dough in her bowl while she listened to the moderator ask, "Let's move on to the topic I think most Americans are especially interested in right now: gun violence. Mr. Shepherd, you've made protecting the Second Amendment rights of citizens one of the central pillars of your platform. Have the recent violent attacks across the country changed your opinion on this matter at all?"

Marcus Shepherd nodded gravely as he answered, "That's an important question, certainly, and I can understand why many Americans are fearful given this rash of violence. The simple truth, though, is this is a question of freedom. Every American citizen should have the right to protect themselves and their families. The bans that have been put in place by politicians like Mr. Santos deny the people of this right."

"Nobody is buying an assault rifle for self-defense," Santos interrupted.

"How else is someone supposed to stand their own against police forces that use military-grade weaponry?" Shepherd asked.

"So you're saying people should fight back against the police?"

"I'm saying the police should be fighting for the people, not the politicians. People should be able to make a stand against laws that take away their basic freedoms.

The moderator tried to restore order but neither candidate was listening to him, at this point. Pat watched intently as Emmanuel Santos stepped out from behind his podium, crossing halfway to Marcus Shepherd's as he said, "And what about the right of the people not to fear for their lives? We've seen violence erupt in schools, shopping malls, movie theaters—places nobody should have to worry they'll be gunned down by some madman."

"Not every gun owner is a violent criminal," Shepherd replied, taking a few steps toward his opponent. "It's like you think people turn into psychotic killers the second they own a firearm."

Santos said, "They do if they listen to people like you. Didn't you just praise the militia in California as freedom fighters?"

"Nobody was killed in that attack. They're frustrated people tired of losing their rights as Christian Americans—"

"Because Christians are the only ones who can be persecuted? What about black Americans, gay Americans, Muslim Americans—shouldn't our laws protect everybody equally?" Santos shook his head, thrusting an angry finger at Marcus Shepherd, and said, "Bigoted idiots like you are exactly the reason our country is falling apart!"

The moderator was shouting, now, standing from his seat and telling the two men to calm down and return to their podiums. Someone in the production team cut the microphones on stage, preventing Pat from hearing their continued argument, but suffice to say it wasn't pleasant. Soon enough they were toe-to-toe, screaming in each other's faces. Santos swung his fist into Shepherd's jaw. It knocked the republican candidate off-balance for a moment but he recovered quickly, storming back at Santos as he threw punches with both fists. The moderator's continuing shouts warred with the shrieks and murmurs from the crowd, some spectators sounding frightened by the spectacle, others egging on their candidate with whoops and curses. Santos tackled Shepherd down to the stage but their brawl continued, the black-clad figures of their respective secret service agents rushing in from either side. It took six of them to wrench the two candidates apart, Shepherd and Santos shouting threats and obscenities at each other even as their security pulled them from the stage and the station, finally, cut the feed.

✪ ✪ ✪

There were a couple televisions available to inmates at the Snake River Correctional Institute, but Blake Davis rarely took advantage of them. He certainly saw no reason to bother watching the presidential debate the night before. He'd lost interest in elected officials about the same time he was convicted a felon. If he couldn't vote anyway, why waste his time paying attention? While the less jaded guys on his cell block watched the debate, Blake holed up in the library with a well-worn copy of *Das Kapital*[9], daydreaming about the better world he'd been arrested for trying to bring about.

It was the next morning, while Blake was eating his breakfast of chalky eggs and burnt toast, that his buddy Carl set his tray down on the table across from him and said, "Yo, did you hear about the debate last night?"

Blake just shook his head and chewed his eggs, uninterested until Carl said, "Santos and Shepherd got in a straight fist-fight."

Blake glanced up at Carl. "You're kidding."

"Not even," Carl answered. "I'm not talking one punch. These dudes were all-out brawling, right there on the stage in their nice suits. The TV network had to cut their feed off and everything. They were, like, two questions in. From what the news was saying after, seems like the rest of the debates are canceled, too. Guess there were riots and fights all over the country all last night. I heard they even had to call out the national guard to quiet things down."

Carl set about dousing his eggs with ketchup and hot sauce. Blake swallowed his bite down with a swig of burnt coffee. "Not much of a loss," he said. "Those things weren't ever real debates, anyway. Just both candidates giving their prepared talking points from the same stage."

Carl chuckled in response, shaking his head. He said, "I'm guessing you'll tell me you wouldn't vote for either of them, even if you could."

---

[9] Book about political and economic philosophy by Karl Marx, considered one of the most influential texts of communist theory.

Blake said, "To be honest, I haven't been paying enough attention to even know."

Although maybe he should start, he thought to himself. He would be up for parole next month, and his lawyer was optimistic about his chances of getting it. Blake had done his best to be a model inmate, and he'd already served six years of his eight-year sentence—with how crowded the prisons were getting, the folks in charge were probably eager to find people they could let out a little early. If presidential candidates were fighting each other on stage, it sounded like the world he'd be going back to was a lot more interesting than the one he'd left. Blake smiled around his next bite, for once not minding the rubbery texture, the bland taste. They'd taken away his vote, but they couldn't take away his voice.

CHAPTER 8

PAT JACOBS HAD COME TO EXPECT HEAT IN THE SUMMER, living in the desert, but by December it was usually more pleasant. Not this year, though. The heat wave that had started back in late November was still going strong, pushing temperatures well above the mid-fifties they could usually expect this time of year. Maybe those left-wing talking heads had been on to something with their talk of climate change, she thought to herself ruefully as she tended to her community's indoor gardens. At least it was much cooler underground. The decommissioned silo where she'd built her home remained a comfortable seventy degrees, even in July and August when the temperature regularly soared over a hundred degrees. Perfect for their plants, too; the arid climate here wasn't the only thing that kept their gardens indoors.

Pat heard footsteps behind her and turned to see Riley crossing through the vegetable beds toward her.

"It's almost six, Pat," Riley said once she saw Pat had noticed her. "Dinner should be ready soon, and that news show you like is about to start, too."

Pat dusted the soil from her hands as she stood up with a groan. "That late already?" she said to Riley. "Time sure flies down here in the garden."

"They're looking great, though," Riley told her with a smile. Riley was one of the newer members of their community. She'd moved in toward the end of last summer, fed up with the commercialized culture and increasing violence in her home city of San Francisco. Between the militias on the right and the violent anti-fascist groups on the left, it was a wonder more people weren't being murdered in the streets of big cities. Riley had worked as a programmer, and her skills for this kind of off-the-grid living had been limited when she first showed up, but she'd been learning quickly and had a natural talent for fixing their air purification and water filtration systems. A good thing, too. There were plenty of people here besides Pat who knew how to keep the gardens growing, but their de facto engineer, Miles, hadn't had many people to help him out until Riley came.

Pat took her spade and shears back to the tool cabinet in the corner then joined Riley on the walkway, passing through the soil beds then the hydroponic bays on their way to the door. "What's on the menu tonight?" she asked while they walked.

"Looked like some kind of stir fry when I popped my head into the kitchen," Riley told her. "Something with pork, maybe?"

"Still learning to identify ingredients, huh?" Pat asked her with a smirk.

"It's all a far cry from the microwave dinners I used to live on," Riley answered. Pat could relate. She'd never taken much interest in cooking. Another big advantage of living in this kind of community: each of them could focus on the things they were good at, dividing their work according to their strengths. Something that might work for the country at large if the people of America could ever stop arguing long enough to learn how to work together.

The pair chatted while they walked up the steps to the third level which housed both the kitchens and the main communal hangout spaces. It was a bit warmer up here, this close to the surface, but still comfortable enough— and a far sight cooler than it must be on the surface. Pat could smell the food as soon as they went through the door, a delicious salty, umami aroma that made her stomach rumble.

"Why don't you go watch your show?" Riley suggested. "I'll check in with the chef, bring you a plate if the food's ready."

"You're an angel, Riley," Pat replied, smiling her gratitude at the younger woman before she went down the hallway to their TV room. She wasn't sure what the space had been in its previous life as a military installation. Some kind of storage space was her main guess, based on the shelves built into three of the four walls. They'd done what they could to give the place a homier vibe, painting over the dull gray of the walls and layering the cement floor with rugs. The furniture was mis-matched and well-worn, mostly picked up from nearby thrift shops, but there were enough seats for twenty or so people, with folding chairs off to the side that could be pulled out if the whole community wanted to watch TV at once. Pat found an empty seat on a couch directly in front of the screen. She was just in time; the program's patriotic intro had just faded into the main anchor at his desk, who gave his usual smiling welcome to viewers, his face turning more serious as he said, "Our top story tonight comes out of eastern Oregon, where the anti-fascist activist group Free the People is in the seventh day of their protest against the arrest of fourteen protesters. Free the People is demanding the release of the prisoners, who have been held without bail at Snake River Correctional Institute since their attack on Republican senator Samuel Evans' campaign office. One staffer was killed and seven more injured in the attack, which caused hundreds of thousands of dollars in damage to the building."

"Whole world's going crazy," Miles muttered from the other side of the couch. "The way things are going it's a wonder we've managed not to all blow ourselves to smithereens."

"Makes me glad we live all the way out here," Pat said, nodding agreement. The TV screen had shifted to footage of the attack's aftermath, firetrucks spraying water into the burning building while two of the staffers who'd been inside looked on, holding each other and sobbing.

Miles said, "Doesn't mean this stuff won't spill out and affect us. If somebody decides to nuke Vegas or LA, we're still in the fall-out zone."

One of the staffers was on the screen now, sitting at the desk beside the anchor while he interviewed her about the ordeal. She was well-spoken but obviously angry; the anchor had to cut her off when she launched into a diatribe about the liberal media, how it was encouraging the people who watched it to commit this kind of violence. As if her side were blameless; Pat had seen plenty of similar interviews from the opposite perspective, after those stand-offs following the assault rifle ban, and the things they'd said had sounded pretty similar. Seemed like everybody felt like they were right and didn't want to listen to anyone who said otherwise.

Pat turned back to Miles and asked, "What do you think it would take, do you think, to get us ready for something like that?"

Miles shrugged, answering, "Not a whole lot, honestly. Heavier shielding on the entrances, a few extra filters in the air filtration systems. We'd need to make some more of our supplies, too—no more heading out for groceries in a nuclear winter." He squinted at her, the look she'd learned meant he was thinking through a puzzle. "Why do you ask? Thinking of turning this place into a survival bunker?"

"Seems to me it wouldn't be a bad idea," Pat answered.

"Can't argue with you there," Miles said. He shook his head at the reporter on the screen then stood, announcing his intention to grab some grub. Riley slid into his vacated seat a minute later, a plate of what looked to be fried rice in each of her hands. If they did have to survive a fall-out at least they'd eat pretty well, Pat thought to herself as she accepted it and forked the first bite into her mouth.

When the cops collared him after the attack on Evans' offices, Blake Davis had expected to spend a few nights in a small town jail. He hadn't thought he'd end up in maximum security, waiting for a trial they seemed in no hurry to get moving, no option to get out on bail even if he'd had the funds for it. But then, he'd thought he'd be facing charges like vandalism, destruction of property, maybe breaking and entering, if they wanted to be tough about it. Certainly, he'd not expected to be counting on a lawyer to get his murder charge downgraded to manslaughter.

He had a decent lawyer, at least, though through no doing of his own. Blake had never had a reason to hire a lawyer before. He'd been afraid, at first, that he'd be at the mercy of the public defenders, a terrifying prospect after the horror stories he'd heard from the other protesters who'd been arrested with him. Luckily, other like-minded groups throughout the country had taken up their cause. Hundreds of protesters had converged on eastern Oregon, picketing outside the courthouse, even closing down the streets of downtown Bend until the police came in and cleared them out. It was one of those groups that had provided the lawyers who'd been representing Blake and his cohorts in their upcoming trials.

Blake was on his way to meet his lawyer now, cuffs around his wrists and ankles as he shuffled down the long gray hallway between the cells and the visiting rooms. At least he didn't have to talk to his lawyer through a pane of safety glass, like he did with other visitors, and the guard left them alone, too, once he'd secured the cuffs on Blake's wrists to the top of the metal table. And his lawyer was a sight for sore eyes, too, with soft brown eyes and a ready smile, her professional attire a welcome relief from the jump-suited prisoners and uniformed guards surrounding him the rest of the time.

"We're making progress on getting a date for your trial," the lawyer told him once they'd gone through their usual greetings. "The discussion right now is whether to try you each separately or as a group."

"Is there an advantage to either?" Blake asked.

"From the state's perspective, a collective trial would be cheaper," his lawyer answered in a cynical tone. "No doubt they're hoping to make a bit of a spectacle over it, too. All the national attention your case has gotten, I have no doubt they're going to televise the proceedings."

Blake asked, "What about from my perspective?"

His lawyer folded her hands on her case file and answered, "It really depends. A collective trial could be a benefit—the jury will need to find all of you guilty to convict one of you. That is, unless you can make a case for yourself that diminishes blame."

"Well I didn't throw the Molotov," Blake answered. "I just thought we were spray painting and throwing rocks. And it was the explosion that killed that staffer, right?"

"The problem is proving it," the lawyer said. "It's unfortunate the security camera footage was destroyed in the fire. We might be able to make a case for it if all of your stories align, though. If we identify exactly who started the fire, we may be able to mitigate the more severe charges against the rest of you."

Blake didn't like throwing the blame on a fellow protester to save his own skin. Not that a twenty-year prison sentence sounded any more appealing.

The lawyer said, "Let's talk through it again. Everything you remember, in order. I'll stop you if I have any questions."

Blake had told her all of this before. He was tired of talking through it, of reliving that night. But he supposed it was a minor annoyance at worst if it could get him out of his cell. He took a deep breath, shifting his hands in their cuffs, and started—again—from the beginning.

CHAPTER 9

David and Marilyn Chandler always made it a point to vote—
in national and local elections, and even in the primaries. It was one message they wanted to make sure they taught their kids: that taking an interest in government was the best way to have your voice be heard. In November of 2032, though, they almost didn't make it to the polls. Not because it didn't seem important—if anything, the extreme difference between the two candidates made voting feel even more necessary—but because they weren't sure if it would be safe. Cancelling the rest of the debates hadn't cooled national tensions at all. Riots and protests had broken out all over the country, and even their quiet corner of Michigan's Upper Peninsula wasn't immune. A Teamster Temple that was to serve as a polling site had been bombed the week before by a group calling themselves Anonymous Anarchists, who wore Guy Fawkes masks[10] in the video they posted online threatening more violence on election day. Just scare tactics, David told his wife at the time, but he couldn't deny the whole thing had been pretty freaked out.

And they weren't the only ones, apparently. As David pulled into the parking lot of the elementary school where they always voted, he saw multiple squad cars had been dispatched. The walk up to the front door was

---

[10] White smiling masks commonly worn by those in the Anonymous movement and protestors. Taken from British figure Guy Fawkes, who famously planned a failed assassination of England's king in the early 17th century known as the Gunpowder Plot.

guarded by rows of police officers in full riot gear, instead of the volunteers and petitioners that normally greeted folks coming to vote.

"Is that supposed to make us feel safer?" Marilyn asked, frowning at the cops, who were holding assault rifles in full view.

"They're a deterrent," David answered as he unbuckled his seat belt. "I'm sure they just want to be prepared for anything."

But Marilyn didn't look convinced, and David didn't feel so confident himself. They sat there for a long moment, waiting until they saw another couple exiting the school safely to finally exit their car and cross the parking lot.

"We'll be in and out in a jiffy," David said to Marilyn, taking her hand in one of his own and squeezing it reassuringly, realizing as he did that it was as much for his own sake as it was for hers.

By midnight on election day, the question of who would be the next president seemed no closer to being answered than it had when polls opened that morning. Emmanuel Santos had been in his California office the entire day with his campaign team, anxiously scrolling the exit poll results, watching CNN for the vote tallies as they came in. He'd taken an early lead on the east coast, with Pennsylvania, New York, and most of New England presumptively coming out in his favor. He'd done less well in the south, though, and as votes came in from the Midwest the balance shifted to his opponent's favor.

"You'll take California for sure," Mehar Ali told him reassuringly. "The whole west coast, in fact. Looks like New Mexico, Iowa, and Minnesota are leaning your way, too."

Santos said, "But the rest of middle America is going red."

"We expected they would," Mehar reminded him. Which was true but didn't make it feel any better to see his opponent's presumptive lead in Nevada and Louisiana, two states where he'd campaigned hard all summer.

"What about Florida?" Santos asked.

Mehar shook her head. "Still too close to call. Seems like that one might take a few days."

"So it all comes down to Florida again," Santos said. He rubbed his eyes wearily; the hours he'd spent staring at screens today had them burning, and his endless pots of coffee had given him a bad case of heartburn, to boot.

"Why don't you go home and get some sleep?" Mehar suggested. "Looks like nothing's getting figured out tonight, at least."

Not a bad idea, in theory, if Santos thought he'd be able to sleep. He had a feeling he'd spend the next few hours laying in his bed, staring up at the ceiling and thinking back on every step of the campaign. Where he could've been stronger. What he'd done wrong. But Mehar was right: he couldn't do anything else here tonight. Emmanuel Santos nodded and stood up, feeling the bones in his spine crack as he stretched them. He had a feeling he had a long few days ahead of him. He should rest while he had the chance.

Three days after the election the Florida election board called the state for Emmanuel Santos. By a ridiculously slim margin, in Marcus Shepherd's opinion; only 147 votes separated him from his opponent.

"They're still counting at least that many absentee ballots!" Shepherd protested in his campaign office when he heard the news. "And the liberal media is already running with the story, acting like there's no question Santos won. Ridiculous! I'm calling the governor right now. Demanding a recount."

"It'll happen automatically," his running mate, Carol Moore, replied. "Anything less than half a percent and they have to recount it—and this is definitely one of those times." She shook her head sadly, said, "This kind of thing is exactly why someone like you needs to be President. Someone who will protect real American democracy."

When the recount results came back a few days later, the balance had shifted—but not by much. Florida now went to Shepherd, but the margin was even slimmer than before, ahead by fewer than a hundred votes. He wasn't surprised to hear that Emmanuel Santos had sued the state, initiating another recount, this one by hand.

Ten days after the election, Emmanuel Santos called Marcus Shepherd at his campaign office.

"It's over, Shepherd," Santos said. "Just got word from the Florida governor. The recount gives me the state again."

Shepherd asked, "By how much this time? Three votes? Who did you bribe to make that happen?"

Santos sighed wearily. Shepherd could just see him shaking his head at what he would no doubt call stubbornness. "Just concede," Santos told him, "This has gone on long enough. It's time to end it."

"I'll never give the country over to you," Shepherd replied. "Florida's obviously just going to keep flopping back and forth. The votes are too messed up to matter. If they call the state for you, I'll take the rest of what I won and make my stand."

Santos said, "You're talking about civil war! You'd really tear the country apart rather than admit you lost?"

It was Shepherd's turn to shake his head; of course Santos wouldn't get it. "It's not about winning," he answered, "It's about the future of the country. America is going to fall apart anyway if I let it fall in your hands. If war is what it takes to keep you from power, that's the way it's gotta be."

With that, he hung up the phone. It was time to prepare his victory speech.

"Hey Pat!" Miles called from the doorway of the indoor greenhouse, "You'd better come into the TV room. They're about to call the election!"

"Took them long enough," Pat answered, wiping her dirty palms against the thighs of her trousers. By this point, election day was a full two weeks ago—and until this morning, the nation had seemed no closer to figuring out who would be their leader come January.

The TV room was packed by the time Pat reached it, all the seats filled and more standing behind them. Seemed like everyone in the community had turned out to see the announcement and the room was loud with voices, most of them sounding bitter and defeated. Pat found Riley near the door and asked her, "I take it Santos won?"

"Looks like it," she replied. "They just officially called Florida. He just gave his victory speech."

It was disappointing news, although not like Pat Jacobs was especially heartbroken. She'd not really been that into either candidate, to be honest, especially after their fist-fight during the debate. Anyone that hot-headed had no place running a country, as far as she could figure. Still, she'd liked more of Shepherd's policies when it came to civil rights. At least Santos had a strong environmental platform; some good could still come out of the next four years.

"Quiet down, guys!" a voice called from closer to the TV, "Something's happening!"

Everyone hushed. Pat maneuvered through them, getting herself a better view of the screen, which now showed Marcus Shepherd speaking from his office. Giving his concession speech, Pat thought at first, until he started to speak.

"My fellow Americans," Shepherd began, "It is clear to me that the electoral politics in this country have once again failed us. My opponent's liberal cronies have stolen the state of Florida with their political maneuvering. The results of the vote counts were no more conclusive than on the previous tallies. This election was rigged from the start and I will not stand for such blatant disregard of the voice of the people. If you look at the popular vote, I have led the polls throughout this debacle. The majority of voters have picked me to lead them. That is the law I must abide. I hereby declare myself the President of the United States of America. I have spoken already with the Commandant of the Marine Corps and he has dispatched troops to take and hold the White House…"

Pat saw Miles standing across the room, his mouth agape. She navigated to the crowd until she was at her side. "You remember those bunker preparations we made?" she asked him in a low voice.

"Of course I do," he answered.

"Let's start getting everything ready to lock down," she told him. "Something tells me things are about to get weird."

On the screen, Shepherd finished his speech but did not cede the podium. Instead, Chief Justice John Roberts slowly crossed the stage in his black robe, Bible in his hand. He looked especially ancient standing next to Shepherd but his voice was clear enough, unwavering, as he said the words swearing Shepherd in as President. The screen split in two, the other side showing a different podium on another stage, where Justice Elena Kagan was holding a Bible for Emmanuel Santos to swear in on. Apparently in a separate America. Pat couldn't pull her eyes away from the display.

Nate Wilson was in the yard of California State Prison, doing his usual workout of deadlifts, when a strange smell reached his nose. An acrid, warm smell, but woody, too, almost like a campfire. He looked up and around, eyes landing on a column of smoke on the horizon in the direction of Sacramento. While he watched, a second column appeared, darker and closer than the first. When he looked behind him, toward the prison, he saw Bill Shaffer jogging across the yard toward him.

"Time to go, buddy!" Bill panted once he was in shouting range.

"Go where?" Nate asked. "We're in prison, in case you haven't noticed."

Bill pointed at the smoke and said, "You saw that, right? From what I heard both Santos and Shepherd declared themselves the president. Military's split branches and the states are picking sides. Apparently things are going nuts out there—looting, riots, the works. Most of the guards took off already, went home to protect their families. Don't think the rest stand much chance of stopping us."

"We're gonna break out?" Nate asked, his head spinning. Part of him thought this had to be a prank, some kind of sick joke, but then he looked back at the black smoke column, looked around the yard. The other inmates were rushing back inside, too, and none of them looked like they planned to stop at the cell block.

Bill said, "Everyone else is. I sure don't want to sit here in prison while there's a civil war on, do you?"

Nate dropped his bar of weights and stood from the bench. "We'll have to find new weapons if we want to start fighting for Shepherd," he said as they crossed the yard.

Bill clapped a hand on his shoulder and said, "Something tells me that won't be a problem." For the first time since their arrest, he looked happy. Nate could relate. They'd only been in here a few months and it already felt too long. But they weren't trapped and useless anymore. Freedom would feel good, but even better was to have a renewed purpose.

CHAPTER 10

UNDER COVER OF DARKNESS, three private jets landed on a small island in the South China Sea. Further out on the water, the lights of aircraft carriers and destroyers from the Chinese Navy twinkled against the night like low, colorful stars. The island itself was dark, for the most part, a few floodlights visible around the doorways of the low concrete buildings. China preferred not to advertise the island's importance. There were advantages to working in the shadows.

The General Secretary was first to arrive. Li Wei was no stranger to this island, had been here only a few months before inspecting their most recent iteration of the H25 stealth bomber. The new models had increased their cruising distance to over 6,000 miles and could carry six hypersonic stealth missiles, ballistic or nuclear. The fleet would soon be moved to an airbase on the other side of the Pacific Ocean, from which the bombers would have easy access to the west coast of North America. He had kept them here temporarily, under the guise of giving a final inspection, though in truth it was in preparation for the meeting that would take place. He did not trust easily, not even those he called allies. Along with the two guards who descended the stairs of his jet with him, Li Wei had dozens of soldiers at the base. All were ready to defend him if the negotiations should turn sour. He was confident as he stood at the side of the landing strip, waiting to meet the others.

The next jet bore the white, blue, and red stripes of the Russian flag and was accompanied by a trio of Mikoyan MIG-35 fighters—an outdated model, the Chinese General Secretary couldn't help but noting. Russia was obviously the weaker partner in this alliance, but this was hardly new information. China had become a pre-eminent global military force. The Russian jet landed while the fighters circled above, lowering its steps for President Putin to descend. He moved like a man younger than his advanced years, spryly navigating the steep stairs and taking powerful strides across the airstrip toward the Chinese leader. His translator, advisors, and guards moved quickly to keep up with him.

The final jet was the smallest, a simple commercial craft bearing no national insignia, and came alone. Kim Yo-Jong, Supreme Leader of the Democratic People's Republic of Korea, was a small woman with a kindly face, but she was no less brutal than her late brother, Kim Jong-Un. If anything she was more dangerous, smarter and craftier; both President Putin and General Secretary Li Wei had received intelligence from reliable sources indicating Kim Jong-Un's death two years ago had been no accident, and Kim Yo-Jong almost certainly had a role in it. Her guards wore simple black attire and were lightly armed. Perhaps rumors the unrest in North Korea were not without merit, President Putin mused idly; he had heard whispers that the elite military and political figures were not best pleased with Yo-Jong's leadership. There had even been word of a coup in progress which he'd dismissed as pure speculation until today.

The three leaders made their introductions but did not linger on the airstrip, all of them eager to begin the negotiations. They crossed quickly to a nearby building and took their seats around the table that had been set up inside the empty warehouse space. Their guards took up strategic positions in the room, translators and advisors standing at the leaders' shoulders. Refreshments were dispensed but sat untouched.

"You have both no doubt heard the news out of America," General Secretary Li Wei said, to start the conversation. "Two presidents have been declared. The people are in open revolt."

"I expect it is only a matter of days until we hear official declaration of civil war," President Putin confirmed.

"Then you know why I have called you here," Li Wei said.

Putin nodded. "The time is right for Project Babylon. I have already begun to mobilize my armies in preparation of your call. Our supply of nuclear armaments is in transit toward the designated launch zone and there is a team of hackers in Moscow right now identifying weaknesses in the American defense system. Which are many—the American leaders have been too concerned with their internal struggles of late to pay much attention to potential threats from outside. I do not doubt we will have full access and control of their electronic systems by the time we are ready to attack."

Li Wei nodded satisfaction. He'd known of these movements already, of course; he had as many eyes on his so-called allies as he did on his enemies. If necessary, China's military had the power to attack the United States on its own and come out victorious. Their seafaring forces were unmatched, nearly 600 warships and submarines in their fleet, five full aircraft carrier battle groups trained to hunt American submarines patrolling shipping lanes. With this, they held full control over the seas on their side of the Pacific, could quickly seize the few American bases scattered throughout the region. But to do so would mean opening his nation up to a counter attack, the fact that had forestalled their taking the nuclear option up to this point. The reason they had joined forces with Russia and developed Project Babylon in the first place.

"The new stealth bombers will be in place at the Pacific bases by week's end," Li Wei told the other leaders. "We have sufficient Dongfeng missiles to neutralize the American Navy before they have a chance to deploy any of their ships in attack. You can focus your firepower on the mainland. My forces will take care of their military outposts."

Supreme Leader Kim Yo-Jong sat patiently while the other leaders discussed, her translator softly muttering their words into her ear. When the two men reached a lull in conversation, she asked, "And what role do you see the People's Republic having in this…Project Babylon? I assume I was not invited here simply to marvel at your military might."

Putin and Li Wei exchanged a glance; both knew this would be the most delicate point of the negotiations. "It is past time to topple the decadent American empire," President Putin began.

"I will make no argument there," Kim Yo-Jong replied.

He went on, "Our plan to do so calls for swift action, but even so the Americans may have time for a retaliatory strike. China and Russia must be protected from this retaliation, to ensure our great nations remain strong in the aftermath, able to expand our control and secure our rightful place as the new powers in the world."

"North Korea has the power to launch nuclear warheads," Li Wei said. "The first strike must come from you. This will keep the American attention off of Russia and China. After the first bombs hit, we will send our troops to their shores disguised as humanitarian aid. They will have no choice but to accept our offer—and this is when we will deliver the death strike, seizing their lands as our own."

Kim Yo-Jong replied, "The Americans will deploy their missiles immediately once we fire. My people will be decimated. You are asking me to sacrifice my nation for this cause."

"A sacrifice that will not go unacknowledged," Putin said. "In return for this, we are prepared to make you the Supreme Leader of the west coast of the United States after we have taken the country for ourselves. You will have a larger nation than the one you rule now."

The North Korean leader contemplated these words, looking from Li Wei to Putin and back. "My people have shown me little respect," she said, finally. "Even now they scheme against me, claiming it to be in my brother's memory. They cannot abide having a woman in charge."

"You will face no such resistance from your new people," Li Wei told her. "Those outdated views will die in the attack, as well."

"I will need assurances, of course," Kim Yo-Jong told them.

Putin said, "And you will have them. Russia has always been true to its word."

Kim Yo-Jong's answering smile, the devious gleam in her eyes, gave her narrow face a wolfish look. Those in her government who opposed her had greatly underestimated her. For that, they would pay the ultimate price. She folded her hands on the table top, leaning in toward the other leaders, and said, "Tell me more about this Project Babylon. It would seem I have some preparations of my own to make."

The three leaders discussed their plans well into the night. They had waited years for this opportunity. There must be no mistakes; there would be no second chances. By daybreak, the three jets were again in the air, bound for their respective countries for their final preparations.

CHAPTER 11

When Blake Davis was released from prison in late September, he'd made a conscious decision to lay low for a while. He was still on probation, and with tensions high as they were, he didn't think it would take much of a slip-up to get him hauled right back to a cell. He attended a few rallies, signed a petition or two, but for the most part he avoided his old crew and steered clear of any demonstrations that looked like they might turn serious. He spent most of his time looking for work, trying to find a place that would hire an ex-felon whose skillset pre-prison had leaned decidedly white collar. Most nights, Blake stayed in, scrolling through social media while he watched the news on his couch. He made an exception on election night, heading out to a nearby bar where he'd once been a regular, though he'd left before midnight, once it was clear no decisions would be made on the presidency before morning.

Two weeks after that the election still wasn't decided, and Blake was still looking for work. He'd decided to expand his usual search radius and drove into downtown Bend, walking all the commercial streets looking for hiring signs, a stack of resumes printed and ready in his backpack. He'd long since given up on being picky about his employment and was filling out an application for a dishwasher position at a dive bar when he heard the noise from the street outside—shouting, honking, a general ruckus that had the bartender craning his neck to stare out the window. It took Blake a few minutes to finish the job application and turn it in. By the time he stepped outside, a crowd had gathered out front of the courthouse down the street. There were cops barring the front door and lining the sidewalk leading up to it. As he got closer, he saw no few people in the crowd were carrying weapons. They'd formed up in front of the courthouse, eying up the police. Blake could hear them shouting but couldn't make out the words. He edged closer, as far as the next corner, where another bystander was watching from a safe distance.

"What's going on?" Blake asked the man.

He answered, "The election results came back. Santos won but Shepherd won't concede. They're both calling themselves the president. Oregon government is backing Santos. Heard there's militias like this popping up all over the state, trying to change their minds. Governor just activated the national guard to help hold them back."

A helicopter whirred by overhead. Blake looked up but he couldn't tell from this vantage if it was police or a reporter. He looked back at the courthouse. Something flew up from the crowd. A bottle, maybe; he was too far to tell for sure. Even from here, though, he could feel the shift in energy, the shouting getting louder, one of the cops pulling out a megaphone, giving the order to disperse.

"Doesn't look to me like they plan on going anywhere," the other man muttered. He shook his head and started walking back down the sidewalk, away from the confrontation. Blake should do the same, especially once the police gave a final warning over the megaphone. Then a shot went off—Blake couldn't tell which side had fired it—and both sides burst into motion, the police firing off tear gas canisters as they moved in on the militia, and while some of them ran, eyes squeezed shut against the gas, others stood their ground, drawing their weapons. His cue to make himself scarce, Blake decided, walking quickly back toward his car as the shouts and gunfire echoed off the buildings behind him.

Sitting behind the desk in the Oval Office for the first time, Marcus Shepherd finally felt like the President. It had taken three days for the marines to secure the building completely. Leftist insurgents had risen up in DC within hours of Shepherd declaring his presidency, led by a group of Democrats from the House and Senate who'd been in the city. Ultimately, though, they'd been no match for the Marine Corps. All of those disloyal politicians were now in custody, the streets of DC empty and silent. Finally, President Shepherd could take up his rightful place in the White House. He sighed his satisfaction as he settled into the plush leather chair then looked out over the room. The White House was theirs but there was more to be done, yet. Sitting across the desk were the Commandant of the Marine Corps, the Vice President, and Shepherd's secretary of defense, who'd come to help him strategize how they would retake control of the country.

"What's our status?" Shepherd asked, folding his hands on the desk.

"We've arrested all the political leaders who oppose your presidency here in the city," the Commandant started. "The Pentagon is in our full control, as well. I also just received word from our troops in Colorado. They've secured NORAD."

Shepherd nodded. "Excellent. How many states have we secured?"

The Defense Secretary said, "We've secured Texas and most of the southeast. New England and New York are holding strong for Santos, and the west coast, too, though our troops have managed to secure a large portion of Northern California.

"Most importantly San Francisco," Vice President Moore added, "Which means we've been able to seize control of Twitter's headquarters. We have a team there now tracing tweets calling for violent action against us. That should help us quell the resistance in the Midwest."

"What's our next step?" Shepherd asked.

"We need to secure the Air Force and Naval bases in the south and Midwest," the Commandant answered.

Shepherd said, "Let's look at where we have Army bases in proximity and send troops to seize them. And we need to send the people a unified message, in all of those states. Twitter's a good start, but let's also identify the stations inciting people to violent rebellion. I want those media outlets seized and everyone replaced."

"I'll get on it right away, Mr. President," Moore replied.

It pained Marcus Shepherd to be even having this discussion. Sanctioning military action against his own people—it wasn't how he'd envisioned his legacy as president beginning. If they acted quickly, though, they could stop the violence, start shifting their attention to healing the damage. Santos had broken the country when he stole the election, but Shepherd vowed he would be the one to fix it.

On a jet flying over the Pacific Ocean, Emmanuel Santos found himself similarly disturbed by his conversation with his cabinet. He hadn't wanted to be on this jet in the first place, but as his advisors had pointed out to him he controlled the air and sea; Shepherd held the ground. No doubt Shepherd already had the Army and Marines looking for ways to eliminate Santos. For the time being, Hawaii had been determined the safest place for him. The only state in the union Shepherd's forces would be unable to reach.

Santos looked through the notes and reports from the briefing again. He'd lost count already of how many times he'd reviewed them. This time, he panned through with an eye for the good news. Governors of New York and Washington holding firm for him; loyalists in Detroit holding out against Shepherd's supporters from northern Michigan; rebellions quelled in Washington and Oregon. In between those bright spots, though, more dire reports. Troops from Fort Sill in Oklahoma were spreading north through the Midwest, arresting the few supporters Santos had in states like Arkansas and Missouri. Rioters in DC had stormed the Capitol building overnight; Santos had seen footage of it burning on the news this morning before he left for the airport. His people were out there; he just had to figure out how to reach them.

"Paratroopers," Santos said suddenly. Beside him, Mehar Ali looked up from her own reading.

"What was that?" she asked.

"We have to send support to New York somehow," Santos went on. "The forces amassing along the southern border are troubling. We can send in paratroopers. If we can break the line and retake Pennsylvania, the governor already pledged his support."

Ali said, "It could work."

Santos went on, "And our colleagues in Washington, we need to extract them somehow. We could send in a SEAL team."

"That's a big risk," Ali answered.

"We can't afford to play it safe in everything right now," Santos answered bitterly. He rubbed his eyes and put the reports aside. It didn't matter how many troops Shepherd threw at him. This was a fight Santos refused to lose.

The engine in Nate Wilson's ancient Jeep Wrangler sputtered and shuddered, even on the flat country road they were driving, but if everything went well it wouldn't need to take them much further. Nate supposed he should consider it a blessing the car had even started after sitting unused for so many months. It couldn't go any faster than 65 no matter how hard he stepped on the gas pedal but not like they were holding anyone up. He'd barely seen another car since they merged onto the freeway. Nate turned to Bill Shaffer in the passenger seat and asked, "You sure we're on the right road?"

"You heard the same report I did," Bill answered. "Marines under siege at California border, at the I-395 blockade."

"It's just that there hasn't been any traffic," Nate said.

"What don't you understand about the word blockade?" Bill replied, starting to sound annoyed. Nate's reply was halted by the sound of heavy traffic behind him and he eyed the rear-view. There were military vehicles coming up fast behind them, at least four that he saw. Nate slowed and pulled over to the shoulder, planning to let them pass, but the vehicles slowed, too, surrounding his Jeep. Two soldiers in Army fatigues got out of the truck. Nate rolled down his driver's side window as they approached.

"No traffic's being allowed to cross the state border," the soldier told him.

Nate said, "That's not where we're headed, Sir."

The soldier studied them suspiciously. No doubt they'd stopped plenty of people coming up here from both sides, Santos supporters joining the attack, folks like him and Bill from the militias who wanted to stand beside the army, lend their guns to the cause. Nate told the soldier, "We're on your side. We heard about the attack and wanted to come join the fight."

"Brought our own guns, even," Bill added from the passenger seat, holding up his rifle. "And we know how to use 'em, too."

The two soldiers stepped away to confer.

"You know that's still technically illegal," Nate said, pointing to Bill's gun. "Maybe it wasn't the smartest thing to point it out like that."

"I didn't want them thinking we were here to mooch on their supplies," Bill muttered back. As he did, the soldiers finished talking, one heading back to the truck, the other approaching the window of the Jeep.

"You can come with us," the soldier said. "Leave the car here. You can come back for it after."

Nate pulled the keys from the Jeep's ignition without a second thought, stopping just long enough to grab his own rifle from the back before running toward the truck.

CHAPTER 12

Kim Yo-Jong was alone in her office when the phone rang.
Her brother's loyalists had intensified their plotting against her in the days
since she'd met with the Chinese and Russian leaders. There had been three
attempts to seize command of the nation's military, though no overt attempts on her life; other than the two guards outside her office door, every
soldier she trusted was guarding the missile launch site, awaiting her orders.
And they would not be waiting much longer, she thought as she picked the
phone up from her desk.

"Babylon must fall," the voice on the other end said.

"I understand," Kim Yo-Jong answered.

There was a click as the call ended. Yo-Jong stood, smoothing her skirt,
then bent to pick up the packed bag waiting beside her chair. Her most valu-
able possessions were already on their way to her new home in Beijing,
her few friends among her people advised to take a vacation, somewhere
outside the country. She'd felt some guilt when she'd agreed to participate
in Project Babylon, remorse for the innocent lives that would be ended, but
the actions of her rivals these past days had further convinced her it was
the only way. They would never stop opposing her; they must be elimi-
nated. They were the ones truly to blame for the deaths that would occur
today. They had pushed her to this, had left her no other choice.

The two guards looked to Kim Yo-Jong when she came through the office door.

"It's time," she told them. "Escort me to the helicopter."

They nodded acquiescence and fell into place, one in front of her and one behind as she made her way up to the landing pad on the roof of the building. She pulled out her mobile as she walked, calling the missile launch center, relieved to hear a familiar voice when the call connected; she'd been careful not to reveal her plans to her opponents, but they had proven crafty in the past. She had worried they would sniff out her intentions, seize missile control, and derail their plans. But it was too late for them to act now. Once events were set in motion, no one would be able to stop them. Kim Yo-Jong gave the order. By the time her helicopter was in the sky, dozens of missiles were flying the other way, bound for targets on the far side of the Pacific. Kim Yo-Jong watched the city of Pyongyang fade into the distance behind her—one last look before its inevitable destruction—and wondered how long it would take the Americans to realize their doom.

Since the election, David Chandler had tried to provide his family as much normalcy as possible. Michigan's Upper Peninsula had thankfully been spared from the bulk of the looting and riots, quickly and calmly declaring themselves loyal to Marcus Shepherd. Early on he'd seen reports from the southern cities like Detroit, where citizens loyal to Santos had stormed the streets, seizing factories and government buildings until the National Guard was brought in to push them out. That was before all the national news outlets were seized, most going dark as both right- and left-wing reporters were arrested by one side or another. The local channel still gave what updates it could, based on the little information that made it out of the big cities.

Not that things were unchanged, even in their rural corner of the country. Schools were still open for the moment, at least in their area, though from what Joe and Lil reported lots of parents were taking the online learning option, keeping their kids at home after seeing the attacks at schools elsewhere in the country. It was slim pickings at grocery stores, too, breakdowns in the supply chain leaving them unable to re-stock after an early wave of panic buying. The Chandlers hadn't yet been forced to start pulling emergency rations from their stockpile at their silo bunker, but David had to admit it was a relief to know it was there. If this went on much longer they'd have no other option. When things had started back in late November David had thought the conflict would be quick-lived but now it was the middle of January, almost two months later, and from what he could see neither side was ready to give up the fight yet.

And that, in David's mind, made it all the more important to keep up their daily routines. Which was why they were eating dinner around the TV, like they always did, the local news playing softly in the background.

"This pot pie's delicious," David complimented his wife. "I didn't realize they had chicken back in stock."

Marilyn answered, "It's from a can. The vegetables, too. But you can't really tell, right?"

"Not at all," David answered, digging in for another bite as he said, "It's a shame we never got that indoor garden going. Maybe if—"

"Dad, look!" Joe exclaimed suddenly, pointing at the TV. The usual anchors had been replaced by a flashing screen, the word WARNING in bold, all capital letters down its center. David grabbed the remote, turned up the volume as a screeching alert sounded in three long bursts. A moment later an automated voice started to speak, the words of the message scrolling across the screen as it said, "This is not a drill. An incoming missile threat has been detected. All citizens should take shelter immediately. If you are not in your home, make your way to the nearest building. Those in multi-story homes should shelter in their basements if one is available. We repeat, this is not a drill…"

David's fork clanked to his plate as the message began to replay. When he looked at his wife she was staring at him, wide-eyed, her face white as a sheet.

"Is this real?" she asked.

"It seems to be."

"Somebody is using nukes?"

"Now, they didn't say that. They just said missiles." But would they say it, David wondered to himself?

"We should go to dad's silo," Joe said, already pushing up from the sofa and running toward his room.

"He's right," David told his wife and daughter, both still sitting, staring at the message on the screen; David turned off the TV and stood from his armchair. "We've gotta move. Pack a bag, quickly—just essentials for a few days. I wanna be on the road in five."

David ran into his bedroom, following his own advice. There'd been no timeline in the message; who knew how much time they had. Could be it was too late already—but if they moved fast enough, maybe they still had a chance.

Two years ago, Pat Jacobs had laughed at Miles when he showed her his new missile monitoring system. He'd been all excited about it, too, how it was linked directly to NORAD's national warning interface, pointing out the details of his code with a child-like glee even though Pat didn't understand the first thing about programming and couldn't really appreciate it. Installing the system had seemed paranoid and useless, when he'd put it in, but now it was clear he'd been prescient[11] in his instincts—and Pat clearly owed him an apology. One she'd have plenty of time to give him, considering they were about to be trapped together for a good long while.

The alarm system continued to blare through the compound as Pat raced toward the main entrance. Miles and his helpers had already lowered the covers on all the air vents to the outside that lacked filtration. Most of

---

[11] Prescient – Having foresight or knowledge of things before they happen.

their people had been inside already but there had been a few out in the surrounding yard, tending to their surface plants, who wouldn't have heard the missile alert. Pat burst out into the open air, running toward the garden as she shouted, "Everybody come inside!"

The figures in the garden straightened, looking at her, though none moved toward her yet.

"Come on!" Pat shouted. "The alarm system's going off. We have to lock down!"

That got their attention. The gardeners started gathering up their things and Pat slowed to a jog, eying up the gardens, wondering if there was any way to save the plants, bring them inside. But there was no telling how much time they had. They'd have to make do with the hydroponic gardens down below.

Pat stopped to catch her breath a moment, fists on her hips as she turned to survey the landscape. A dust plume caught her eye on the horizon. Pat squinted at it as it materialized into a vehicle, some kind of old Jeep, she thought, eying the canvas top. By the time the gardeners had started making their way back toward the entrance, the Jeep was close enough Pat could see two men inside, driver and passenger both wearing camo-print hats; the passenger seemed to be holding a rifle. Pat trotted out to meet them.

"Who are you?" she shouted as the driver stepped out of the vehicle.

"Name's Nate Wilson," the driver shouted back. "This is my buddy Bill. We were driving down the road when we heard the announcement. We're just looking for some shelter."

Pat looked back toward the door of her compound, at her people scurrying down into the safety of its corridors. Everyone who lived here now had been here a year or more. They knew each other, had a community. These men could be anyone. No knowing if they were violent, if they would pull their weight. But then, if all these warnings were right, she couldn't very well send them away with a clear conscience.

"Leave the gun in the car," Pat shouted to them.

The passenger held his rifle close to his chest protectively, shouted back, "What if we need to defend ourselves?"

Pat said, "If you don't think my home's safe enough for you, you can find somewhere else to shelter."

Except the closest town was a solid half-hour drive away and nothing much but desert in between. Either the men knew that or they didn't want to take the risk. A minute later the rifle was locked securely in their Jeep and Pat and the men were descending the steps down into the compound, Pat pausing only long enough to shut and secure the main door behind them.

✪ ✪ ✪

In the war room of Pearl Harbor Naval Base, President Santos and his cabinet members listened in tense silence to the defense's secretary's side of a phone conversation.

"No scheduled strikes?" the Defense Secretary asked. "You're sure of it?"

He paused, listening to the response, then nodded, said, "Excellent. Thank you, Ambassador."

"Well?" President Santos asked as his defense secretary hung up the phone.

"Our sources in South Korea say the same as the ones in China," the Defense Secretary answered. "No reports of activity around North Korean missile bases."

"The launch report has to be an error," the Vice President concluded.

"I'd like to be sure," President Santos said. "Any response from North Korea?"

The Vice President answered, "Nothing yet, sir."

There had been errors before, Santos knew, erroneous reports that there were missiles headed for this territory or another. Or it could be a trick by Shepherd, some ploy to make him run scared, and—what? Discredit him? Lure him into an ambush?

"Scan the water again," Santos ordered. "Shepherd took a couple of our Naval bases along the southern coast. It's possible that…"

A strange sound caught his ear, then, interrupting his train of thought. The others heard it, too, all of their eyes drawn toward the ceiling by the low humming whine that seemed to be getting louder. Exponentially so. Like a plane, maybe, but coming in too fast to land. Santos rushed to the window to see what was going on now. When he saw the missile growing on the horizon he turned, running out of instinct, knowing it was useless even as he did. The world exploded in flame just as he reached the door. His death was instantaneous, his body vaporized to ashes as a mushroom cloud bloomed over what was once Pearl Harbor.

CHAPTER 13

IT WAS SHEER LUCK THAT VICE PRESIDENT CAROL MOORE was at the Cheyenne Mountain Complex in Colorado when the bombs hit. President Shepherd had sent her to monitor their defenses at NORAD. The army had seized it in short order at the start of the conflict but there were pockets of liberal resistance in cities like Denver and Boulder that Shepherd had found worrying. They'd been deep in their discussions of how to best deal with this resistance when the alarms started blaring and Carol was rushed through the halls, deeper into the complex, secured inside the facility's nuclear bunker with the rest of their troops stationed there. She'd been in denial, telling herself it was just a false alarm, until the walls shook and the lights sputtered out. They'd huddled together around portable battery-powered lamps while the engineers tried to figure out why the emergency backup generators hadn't kicked on like they should have. As the hours dragged on Vice President Moore had tried to sleep, knowing she would need a clear head for whatever came next, but her mind wouldn't stop racing with questions. How many bombs had there been? How many dead—and was the President among them?

She had no sense of how much time had passed when the overhead fluorescent bulbs sputtered back to life, Moore and the soldiers around her blinking up and around. She stood and stretched, saw the army commander standing by the door, talking to one of the engineers, and made her way to them in time to hear, "...EMP attacks along with the nuclear strikes. We also have reason to believe they've seized control of whatever computers are still operating on the surface through cyber attacks, but there's no way to confirm until we can make contact."

Moore asked, "So what does that mean for us? Are our electronics useless?"

The engineer turned his attention to her and shook his head. "Anything inside the bunker was protected. Now that we have the back-up generators running we have full control of our environmental systems, lights—"

"What about the missile launch controls?" Moore asked.

The engineer glanced at the commander before answering, "Fully operational. At least the ones at this location."

Moore nodded. Her mind still felt vague, hazy, as though this was all a terrible dream, but she forced herself through it, telling herself her nation needed her. Somebody had to pick up the pieces. She took a deep breath and asked the question she'd been avoiding, dreading the answer to. "Do we have an idea what's going on in the rest of the country? How many missiles were there?"

"We don't know all the specifics yet," the commander answered. "We've confirmed strikes on Los Angeles, New York, and DC. We've tried to reach the President in the Emergency Operations Center but we're getting no reply. Their electronic systems may have been shut down, like ours were."

Or he might be dead, Moore thought. The protections in the emergency bunker under the White House were outdated, unlikely to hold up against a direct nuclear blast. Moore hoped she was wrong, said a quick prayer for President Shepherd's survival. But even if he was alive, he was out of contact, unable to lead. For the moment, at least, it fell to her.

"Do we know who sent the missiles?" Moore asked.

"North Korea," the army commander answered.

"In that case, show me to the launch controls," Moore answered. "Send a message to South Korea and China warning them to pull their troops back from the border. And let's see if we can get through to any of our aircraft carriers. This is bigger than Shepherd against Santos, now. Hopefully they'll see that."

"Aye, sir," the commander replied, leading the way out of the room and down the hallway, eerie in the flickering emergency light. Washington, LA, New York—and how many more? Vice President Moore set her jaw to a grim line. The time for grieving would come. First, she would defend what of her country was left.

The United Nations had still been in session in New York; most of the delegates were presumed dead with the city now in ruins. When an emergency session was called in the days after the attacks, most nation's leaders came to Geneva in person, the looming threat of world war too great to leave in someone else's hands. As the leaders milled about in the minutes before their meeting, President Putin and General Secretary Li Wei met eyes across the room, both of them drifting to a quiet spot along the wall.

"We shouldn't be seen together long," Putin said. "People will talk."

Li Wei answered, "They have their suspicions already. But it will make no difference. Project Babylon is too far along now to be stopped."

"So you have had success in South Korea?" Putin asked.

"And Japan," Li Wei replied. "Both were quick to surrender the moment my fleet threatened them."

Putin said, "Japan wasn't part of our initial plan."

Li Wei said, "They are allies of the United States. They would have attacked us in short order if I hadn't acted first."

The two men surveyed the room as they spoke, the voices pitched low, their demeanors casual. The leaders of France, Italy, and Canada were standing nearby, out of hearing range, heads bent together, intent on their conversation. The same seemed to be true throughout the room. Everyone too caught up in their own schemes to be concerned with anyone else's.

"You've kept back enough troops for the next stage of Babylon, I hope?" Putin said.

Li Wei nodded. "Of course. I'll announce my plan today to send humanitarian aid. The force will be on its way by nightfall, with full world approval."

Putin said, "My sources in America tell me you will not meet much resistance. Both presidents are confirmed dead, most of their major military outposts destroyed. The few missiles they still had they used in their attack on North Korea."

"I am confident my troops will prevail over whatever sad resistance they send to meet us," Li Wei replied.

A bell chimed from the assembly room. The assembled leaders began to slowly drift toward the door. Putin couldn't help but pity them as he watched them file into their seats. They actually believed they still had control. And that arrogance, it would be their undoing.

Oregon had been spared any direct missile impacts but Blake Davis wasn't naïve enough to think himself safe. He knew about nuclear fall-out, radiation, the way it was spread and carried. He hunkered down in his house overnight and when the sun rose and the power was still blacked-out, his cellphone still without a signal, he went out to his car and was relieved to find it started. An automated signal on an AM radio band told him a safe zone had been identified along the Pacific Coast and Blake took off west. He was the only car on the road for most of the trip—or the only active car, at least; he twice had to find alternate routes through towns when he came upon a patch of abandoned cars on the highway, their drivers nowhere in sight. Traffic increased the closer he got to the safe zone, though, a reassuring sign, even if the traffic backup had him at a standstill for well over an hour. He flipped through the radio dial, eager for news, finding only static on every channel except the emergency alert.

The sun was already low in the sky by the time he was directed to the parking lot of a strip mall. Newport, the town was called, one of those quaint tourist towns along the Pacific Highway that dotted the Oregon coast. Though it didn't look so peaceful now. White tents had been set up on the beach, National Guardsmen directing lines of frightened citizens between them, more going in and out of the buildings of the strip mall, milling around in the parking lots. Blake trotted up to the closest and asked him, "Where should I go?"

"Are you from outside the safe zone?" the guard asked in response.

Blake said, "I think so. Eastern Oregon."

The guard nodded and pointed to the beach. "Head down to those tents. They'll check you out for signs of radiation poisoning, take you through whatever decontamination…" The guard trailed off, squinting at something along the coastline. Blake followed his eyes, putting up a hand to shield them from the glare of the setting sun. There was something crossing the water, certainly, though just a smudge still from this distance.

"What is that?" Blake asked the guard.

"Ships, it looks like," he answered, though he didn't sound too sure of himself.

Blake said, "American Navy, do you think?"

"Or could be the Chinese ships," the guard answered. "We got word they're sending aid."

"China's sending aid?" Blake asked.

"Weird, right? Not who you'd expect to give a helping hand. To be honest, though, how thin our resources are stretched, I'm not going to question it. We could use all the help we can get."

Blake watched the ships while he made his way down to the beach, inserted himself in the back of the line weaving toward the tents. He could make the ships out more clearly as they neared. They looked like transport vessels, he saw now, a half-dozen or so all loaded with shipping containers. Blake's interest in them waned as he progressed further in the line, where the National Guard members were interspersed with medical professionals in full hazmat suits. Was he contaminated, Blake wondered? Would he feel it if he were? The people around him were asking themselves the same questions, he could tell, their eyes darting nervously toward the tents just like his, their faces tight and pale, jumping every time someone in the line coughed.

A loud noise drew his attention down the beach, to the nearby port. The Chinese ships had finished docking, even more massive than they'd looked from out at sea. One of the shipping containers was open, a bunch of men in uniform coming out of it, which Blake registered as strange but not alarming until a second container opened and a tank rolled out.

"It's not aid!" Blake shouted. "The ships. It's an attack!"

The National Guard members around him jumped into motion, drawing their weapons and forming a line. The other people in line started running the other way, screaming as they scattered down the beach, but Blake found himself frozen in place, staring at the tank as its turret cannon turned their direction and fired.

CHAPTER 14

BLAKE DAVIS HAD ALWAYS THOUGHT OF HIMSELF AS BRAVE, the kind of person who would put himself in harm's way to save others. When that first tank blast ripped out over the Oregon coast, though, he'd turned tail and run, just like everyone else in that frantic crowd—straight past his car, weaving between the traffic waiting on the highway, pausing just long enough to bang on a couple hoods and tell the people inside to get out, save themselves, before sprinting into the trees on the other side at a speed he didn't know his legs could reach. Eventually he'd found his way to a clear road and flagged down an SUV, a family who'd been on their way to the safe zone when they'd seen the explosions on the horizon and sensed things weren't as safe as they'd been told. Their plan now was to head east into Idaho then turn north, drive to the Canadian border. Even if Canada wouldn't let them in, the family figured, at least Idaho seemed safe. For now. Blake couldn't argue; it was a better back-up plan than anything he'd managed to come up with.

When they reached I-90, it became clear they weren't the only ones who'd had this idea. The lines of traffic on the highway were uncomfortably similar to the ones he'd found on the Oregon coast, down to the National Guard members stationed periodically down the shoulder. The Canadian border was closed, they learned when they flagged down one of those guards, but there was a safe zone up ahead, rows of those same white tents, the same hazmat-suited doctors walking between them. This time, though, there was no interruption of gunfire. Blake and the family he'd traveled with were split up during the processing. He was examined, showered, handed new clothes, and loaded into the back of a canvas-topped truck with a half-dozen strangers. The truck dropped them off at a motel a few miles down the interstate. It was run-down, not a place Blake would've chosen driving by, but as he walked into his room he was just happy to be out of the cold and wind. He collapsed onto the creaky bed, too exhausted to do anything but fall into a fitful sleep.

A knock on his door woke him the next morning. Blake answered groggily, forgetting for a second where he was and why, the previous day's events coming back to him gradually as he crossed to the door. The man standing outside was definitely military, though something about the uniform looked different. Blake realized what it was when the man turned, showing a Canadian flag on his left arm.

"Good morning, sir," the man said. "Sorry for waking you. I'm with the Canadian Armed Forces. We're preparing a strike on the Chinese forces in Washington with our European allies."

Blake said, "They're in Washington, too?"

"And California," the soldier confirmed. "I'm looking for abled-bodied Americans who want to join in and help us retake the territory."

"I don't have any military experience," Blake told him. "Never even fired a gun, in fact."

The soldier answered, "That's no problem. Combat isn't the only way to help."

In the parking lot behind the soldier, fat snowflakes were falling into piles already forming on the ground. Was it snowing in Oregon, too? He pictured other survivors from the attack on the safe area struggling onward through the cold. Pictured what he'd be doing if that family hadn't stopped to give him a ride. Somebody had to help them.

Blake said, "In that case, where do you need me?"

"Just follow me, sir," the soldier answered. Blake turned back to the room to grab his things before he remembered everything he owned was back in Oregon. Even the clothes he was wearing weren't his. Prison all over again, he thought to himself with a rueful smile as he pulled the door shut and followed the soldier across the parking lot.

Some of the folks in Pat's community claimed they could feel it when the bomb went off. Riley was one of them. There'd been a vibration, she insisted, a shaking that came up through her feet, that she felt in her heart. And she wasn't the only one. Pat had heard others in their community talking about it in passing, some even saying they'd heard the sound of the detonation. Pat suspected they were making it up; Los Angeles was the closest city to be nuked, they learned when news updates started coming through on the radio a couple weeks ago—about a week after the bombs dropped— and that was almost 300 miles away. Surely it was impossible to hear or feel anything from that distance. But she wasn't going to argue over it. Let them process what was happening however they needed to.

Pat wasn't completely sure why she still listened to the news updates but she couldn't stop herself. Every time she found herself with free time between tasks she would feel this draw to what used to be their TV room, where they'd set up a dusty old boombox in place of the now-useless television, continuously playing the one AM station they'd found that came through reliably down here in their bunker. The list of cities destroyed was the only information the people sending the radio broadcasts seemed to know for sure. Early on the report said the Chinese were sending aid. Two days later, that turned into the Chinese were attacking, that their troops had seized northern California and most of Oregon. Since then, things got even more chaotic. One eyewitness would come on saying the US army troops remaining on the west coast were holding the invading forces at the California border, another one two hours later insisting he was wrong, the Chinese were pushing east into Nevada, their sights set on NORAD in Colorado. She found herself longing for a TV news report, to see even one second of live footage that could help her picture how things were out there, but from what Miles had explained to her TV broadcasting equipment contained too many complex electronics. It was probably completely fried by the wave of EMP attacks. Until they were to rebuild, radio was likely as high-tech as their media was going to get.

If troops had come through, they hadn't bothered Pat's community. Would they have heard their passage, felt the rumble of boots and tanks above like her companions had claimed to feel the bomb explosion? She had no way to know, and no other way to confirm what was happening outside, above them. There was a scientist who'd get on the radio broadcast periodically to announce areas that had been declared safe zones, others that were confirmed radioactive, but he hadn't yet said anything about her corner of Nevada one way or another. Pat didn't plan to open the door to the outside until she was sure it was free of fall-out. The people in her community had put their trust in her to keep them safe. She wouldn't make any decision lightly if it would put them at risk.

It was still early enough when Pat walked into the old TV room with her morning coffee that she expected to be the only one there. Instead, she saw Nate Wilson sitting on the couch in front of the entertainment center. Nate was the only one in the community who seemed as hooked on the news reports as much as she was. Everyone else's interest had wanted after the first couple of days—even Nate's companion Bill, who'd settled in nicely with the rest of the community, easing Pat's initial fears about welcoming strangers into their midst—but if anything, Nate was in here even more often than Pat was. Right now, he was perched forward with his forearms resting on his knees, staring at the radio with an intensity that made Pat think of her uncle listening to Dodgers games when she was a kid, how he would yell at anyone who walked in front of him, like he thought he could really see the plays if he stared hard enough. Pat looped around behind Nate, just in case, sitting on the other end of the couch. It was the doctor on the radio now, giving advice on common materials that provided protection from radiation.

Pat wanted to ask if she'd missed anything important but Nate didn't look like he was in the mood for conversation. And he was annoyed with her, she knew. Nate wanted to join up with the US forces fighting along the California border, eager to defend his country. Twice Pat had pulled him away from the main door, which was thankfully locked with a passcode only the core community members knew. The last time, he'd shouted at her that they were all cowards, hiding down here afraid for their lives when they should be fighting for their country. Pat had countered that none of them would be much help if they died of radiation poisoning. He'd apologized for yelling at her later that day and hadn't brought up leaving since, but he was clearly still frustrated by their lack of action.

The usual news voice took over the broadcast, thanking the doctor for his input then saying, "We have new reports coming in from the southern border of the United States. Armed forces from several South and Central American nations entered Texas this morning and are pushing north, planning to join the American resistance fighters currently fighting the advance of Chinese forces through Arizona. The army has been holding the border between the United States and Mexico for a few days but was prevented from going further by a dust storm outside the remains of Dallas, which they were concerned could be spreading radioactive fall-out over…"

Pat saw Nate shifting out of the corner of her eye. She looked at him and shook her head, saying, "Don't even ask. Unless you heard that doctor earlier saying this area's safe, nobody's going anywhere."

"The door would only be open for a second," Nate argued. "Just long enough for me to slip out then you could close it again. I mean, if those troops are marching through here—"

Pat said, "He said Arizona, not Nevada."

"Close enough. Anyway, isn't Arizona closer to LA than we are?" Nate said.

"Parts of it," Pat answered. "But it's not just about distance. And don't you try to tell me you understand how nuclear fall-out works. None of us really knows how bad it is out there."

Nate folded his arms and sat back, seething. On the radio, the news voice was still talking about what was going on in Arizona; at last report, besieged American resistors were pinned down by Chinese forces in Phoenix. Pat sighed and sipped her coffee, listening until the topic changed to news out of the northeast. Those states had been hit hardest by the attack, and Pat knew she should give them the same attention and sympathy, but her brain couldn't handle the full scope of the destruction, yet. The fights in Arizona were something she could process. It was harder to imagine the flattened New York City skyline, the smoldering remains of Boston, the scorched earth in DC where the White House used to be.

When Pat looked at Nate again, he was still sulking. "You know most people would feel lucky right now," she said. "You might be dead already if you hadn't found our place when you did."

Nate made a sour face, wanting to argue, but finally he uncrossed his arms with a sigh and said, "I know. I just feel so useless."

"We all do," Pat told him. "Look, if those troops think it's safe enough to come through this area, or that doc on the radio says it's okay—"

"You'll let me go join them?" Nate said, perking up, looking so much like an excited kid Pat couldn't help smiling.

"Heck, I might come with you," Pat answered. And she wasn't joking, either. She wanted just as much as he did to fight for their future. She just wanted to make sure there were people left to live in it.

CHAPTER 15

WHEN CAROL MOORE HAD AGREED TO BE MARCUS SHEPHERD'S Vice President she'd known there was the potential she'd have to one day lead the United States. But Shepherd had been young and healthy, and she'd had no reason to believe this possibility would become reality. Certainly not less than a year after the election, or in the aftermath of an attack that had killed millions of Americans and left millions more huddled, scared and homeless, in safe zones and bunkers scattered across the country. She'd long considered herself a good leader, coming up through grassroots political organizations just as Shepherd had, but she wasn't sure any experience could have prepared her for the daunting task before her. At least the conflict that had laid the way for this whole mess seemed to have died down. Even those who had violently opposed Shepherd—and Moore, too, by extension—seemed grateful simply to have someone to lead through this invasion. She'd been quickly sworn in as acting President the day after China's troops landed on the coast, and in the months that followed no one had come forward to challenge or argue the title.

Meeting with world leaders was one thing Moore hadn't prepared for in her life as a community organizer. In the two days since China agreed to a temporary cease fire, she had spent most of her time reading up on negotiation tactics, studying what she could of Chinese history. In normal times, there would be experts at her side, giving her the information she'd need to make sure this conversation ended in a peace treaty. Those experts were probably dead, though, and if they were alive she had no way of reaching them. Even the internet was out of her reach; she was truly on her own.

But no, President Moore told herself, not completely alone, however it felt. America—or whatever she should call the remains of the nation—still had allies. It was thanks to them a cease fire had been called in the first place. The combined South American force that came up through Mexico had retaken Arizona and Texas, holding the invading Chinese troops at the California border. The UK and France, meanwhile, had sent their forces to join the Canadian army in the north, preventing the invasion from spreading beyond Oregon and Washington. Both efforts were partially self-serving, Moore knew—the Canadian effort more obviously so than that of their South and Central American neighbors—but she was still grateful. Thanks to them, there was a temporary peace. It was up to her, now, to make sure that lasted.

President Moore smoothed her skirt over her hips, squared her shoulders, and strode through the door into the negotiation room. Li Wei of China was already seated within, as was their negotiator from NATO. The negotiator was Japanese. Moore wasn't sure if that would work for her or against her. The Japanese had been long-time allies of the United States and had their own bone to pick with China based on recent events, but they were also technically aligned with the Chinese, now, even if by force rather than by choice. Negotiators were supposed to be impartial, but she couldn't see how anyone truly could be, facing down a world war.

Moore and Li made their introductions through the NATO translator then took their seats across the table from each other. They were meeting in a city building in a small town on the Washington/Idaho border. Its laminate floors and well-worn furniture were strangely comforting to Moore as she settled into the space. She'd done most of her political work in spaces more like this one than the sleek, well-appointed rooms she'd seen world leaders meeting in on TV.

"Let's not draw this out more than necessary," Li said to start the negotiation. "Our forces are well-supported on the west coast. Even with the support of your allies, you will not be able to force us out easily."

"America has never ceded its land to an enemy force," Moore answered.

Li said, "And it has never been the target of nuclear weapons. Things change, Madame President."

Moore clenched her hands in her lap, struggling to keep the rage from showing on her face. She couldn't prove that the Chinese had been behind the missile attack from the now-obliterated North Korea, but it was a suspicion that had been on her mind since the first tanks rolled onto American soil up and down the coast. That was reason enough for rage, but it was worse to realize he was right. All the skirmishes so far along the border had resulted in stalemates, gains of at most a few feet at a time, not enough to justify the number of death on both sides. America had suffered enough losses already. She couldn't afford to let pride delay them from rebuilding any longer. Even so, President Moore's mouth twisted up in distaste as she told Li Wei, "I'm willing to cede the former states of California, Oregon, and Washington to you permanently—with conditions, of course. The most important being that any American citizens currently in those areas will be given time and freedom to gather their belongings and safely evacuate."

Moore watched Li Wei's face as the translator repeated her words. Her blood boiled when she saw his smug smile. She didn't have to speak Chinese to hear his condescending tone as he said, "I don't know that you're in any position to be putting conditions on our treaty."

"We'll fight you to the last man if we have to," Moore replied, her voice steely.

Li Wei studied her for a moment. When he finally nodded, it was an indulgent gesture. "Alright," he said. "What are your other…conditions?"

He knew he was winning; that was what galled President Moore the most. But her duty now was to her people, to their survival. Balances of power always shifted; nothing was permanent. Moore told herself this, firmly, as she leaned into the table and began to lay out her demands.

After five months underground, both supplies and patience were running thin in the Chandler family survival silo. By David's estimates, there was enough food left in the pantry to keep all four of them fed and healthy for another two weeks—three, maybe, if they tightened their rations—and their fuel stores for the generators wouldn't last much longer.

So it was a relief when the first week of May brought two pieces of good news. The radiation levels in Michigan had fallen to habitable levels everywhere except the immediate area of Detroit, and a peace treaty had been signed between the remains of the United States and the invading Chinese army. The second point was of less immediate concern to David, the fighting contained to the western part of the country even when it was at its most intense, but it was still a reassuring sign. Maybe—finally—they could start to rebuild, create a new society. At the very least, he figured, at least he felt comfortable leaving the silo for the first time since the bombs dropped. Though not quite comfortable enough to take his family back out into the world, yet. Not until he'd seen the state of things for himself.

After the months sitting unused, David's car wouldn't start until he pulled out the portable jump starter. It felt strange climbing into the driver's seat. The motions were familiar but in a nostalgic way, like playing a game as an adult that you used to play as a kid. He didn't see any other cars on the roads nearby but he still put on his seat belt before sliding the car into drive and looked both ways before he turned out onto the main road, giving into the old instincts, however unnecessary they seemed.

David saw a few signs of life on his drive into the closest town but he didn't spot any actual other people until he came up to the local Catholic church. The white cross on its steeple gleamed like a beacon in the bright springtime sunshine and the bushes and flowers planted around its perimeter were neat and well-tended, not the abandoned sprawl he'd seen in other yards he passed. When he got to the front of the building he saw the large wooden doors were propped open, a handful of people milling about just within. David pulled over to the curb and cautiously got out of his car. He'd seen enough apocalyptic movies for images to scroll through his head of violent marauders, bands of cannibals preying on innocent survivors. One of the figures within saw David and stepped out, into the light, revealing his priest's attire. Newly reassured, David met him on the steps up to the entrance.

"Those people," David asked, pointing at the others inside. "Are they other survivors?"

The priest shook his head and said, "They're missionaries from Colombia. They've come to scout locations for a mission, see which areas have the most needs. From what they tell me there are teams like them around the nation, from all over the world. All here to help us rebuild."

It was a touching gesture, David had to admit, but he felt his heart sink slightly. It was a question he'd been turning over in his head for months: how many of them were left?

"But you're the priest here," David asked.

The priest smiled. "I am. Father Donovan's the name."

David said, "And have you seen any other…that is, other than the missionaries, do you know…"

He couldn't find the words to ask the question, his conversation skills stunted by the months talking to no one but his own family. Father Donovan, though, took his stuttering in stride.

"I've seen several from my flock," he said, "And a few strangers, like you. There are survivors, my son, and through God's grace I know we can endure." Father Donovan paused, looking back through the church doors, then asked David, "Would you like to come inside, share our meal? It's nothing fancy—canned meats, a few fresh vegetables from the church garden—but there is plenty to go around."

David was tempted, the offer to socialize again after so long almost too sweet to resist, but then he thought of his family waiting back at the silo. They would be worried about him, wondering what he'd found. He shook his head, said, "My wife and kids are waiting for me."

Father Donovan nodded. "Well, the doors here are always open. And we'll be resuming services come Sunday, with the help of the missionaries. You're welcome to bring your family."

"I will," David told him. "Thank you, Father."

It wasn't until David was driving away that he realized he had no idea what day of the week it was. Sunday could be tomorrow, for all he knew. But there had to be something keeping track of dates down in the silo, he told himself, too excited to share his news with Marilyn and the kids to turn back now.

CHAPTER 16

CONSTRUCTION ON THE NEW UNITED NATIONS HEADQUARTERS IN PARIS hadn't yet been fully finished, but the building was complete enough it could be used to host a meeting—and they couldn't afford to wait any longer. Half a year had passed already since the attack on the former United States, which most people had now taken to calling World War III, though others still referred to it as the Second American Civil War. Whatever history would name it, it was the closest humanity had yet come in its history to complete self-annihilation. The dead were still being tallied in the former United States and the ruins of North Korea, but even conservative estimates put it over 100 million; more than nine million had died in New York City alone. Far more lives than had been lost in World War II, and how many more would have been lost if other nations got involved, launched their own missiles? That didn't even count the chaos that had been caused around the world by the sudden elimination of the United States from the global economy. The ramifications would be felt for generations.

The walls were up in the General Assembly chamber but the space hadn't yet been painted or furnished, the floors and walls both a drab cinder-block gray. Folding chairs were set up in front of portable metal tables where, eventually, rows of hardwood desks would rise in rings from a plush carpet, a roll of which was propped in the far corner of the room. The delegates were too concerned with the matters up for discussion to pay much attention to their surroundings. However dire the situation in the former United States, the world had been lucky; the destruction was fairly contained. It was up to them, now, to ensure such a thing would never happen again. If it did, they may not be able to recover.

"A world government is still the only logical answer," the UK delegate insisted, for the third time since they'd begun the conversation. "So long as nations have control of their own territory and military forces, conflicts of this nature are bound to happen. We've attempted diplomatic solutions and interventions for decades. We've tried asking nations, politely, to disarm their nuclear weapons, or at the very least not to use them. We can see now how effective that is."

"The British representative is naïve," Turkey's delegate responded. "Armed conflicts won't just vanish because the world's military has a central authority. We'll just see the formation of more militias, of terrorist organizations—all the dangerous groups that history has shown always form to fill such voids of power."

"National militaries will still have full freedom to defend their people," the Australian delegation jumped in. Like the UK, they'd be one of the more vocal supporters of the world government.

The Chinese delegate asked, "And who defines the difference between defense and offense?"

"A council of nation-states, like this one," the UK delegate said, his tone weary; this was not the first time these points had been argued over.

China's delegate, however, still wasn't convinced. And he wasn't the only one. Other heads nodded around the room as he asked, "What if there is a civil war? Uprisings, revolutions—who decides the victor, in these cases? Who determines which side the world military backs?"

South Africa's delegate added, "I'm also concerned about the reach of this hypothetical World Government. Clearly it must have the ability to write laws or else it won't have the power to prevent conflicts. But what aspects of life will they have control over? What is to stop the imposition of laws that dictate how citizens worship, how they make a living, how they educate their children? All too often in the past we have seen individual rights trampled on in the name of progress."

The Australian delegate said, "The people of each nation will have the right to dictate how they live their lives, like they always have. If anything, they'll be better able to make their own decisions without the threat of being gunned down in the street, and without other nations meddling in their affairs."

"Unless the world government deems them a threat to world peace, I imagine," the Russian delegate added. He'd been fairly quiet to this point but his few comments made it clear which side of the issue he stood on. Now, he cleared his throat, folded his hands, and said, "Surely if there were to be a genocide, for example, the world government would step in. But where does the line of human rights intervention get drawn? How long will it take the capitalist nations to determine communism is a threat to world stability, as they have in the past, and send the world army to impose their ideals in Russia or China?"

"The economy will continue to operate as it always has," the annoyed British delegate replied.

Russia's delegate responded, "Impossible! Who will pay this military? Where will the equipment be produced? This will certainly have economy impacts. To say otherwise is to be blind to reality."

A few heads nodded thoughtfully at the Russian delegate's questions, but no few looked skeptical of the motive behind the argument. Why was Russia so insistent on maintaining control of their military? Most of the nations with representatives here didn't have their own store of nuclear weapons; they would be helpless against an attack if one came. Before, they'd all lulled themselves in to false senses of security by saying surely no nation would make such a strike, take such a risk, certainly not unprovoked. That illusion had been shattered when the first bomb struck. If the United States had still existed, perhaps their delegate would have stood to speak about freedom, of the rights of nations to defend their own borders, the rights of their people to choose their own leaders. But the specter of the once-great nation only seemed to suggest what became of such a stance. Their freedom had been their undoing. The great experiment had failed.

The delegates debated well into the evening. A blind vote as they were preparing to end their first day of discussion revealed only ten nations outright opposed the formation of a world government.

President Putin was unsurprised when he read his delegate's report that night. He had seen people before giving up their rights in exchange for safety. The more people's lives were threatened, the more they would sacrifice. Putin spent much of that night contemplating unexpected consequences. He had not spent all those years putting together Project Babylon, toppling an empire, only to have another pop up in its place. He checked the time; it was late, and later still in Beijing, but he knew Li Wei would be awake to take his call. Perhaps there was still a way they could turn this situation to their advantage.

CHAPTER 17

DAVID CHANDLER HAD LAUGHED OUT LOUD when Marilyn suggested they take a family vacation.

"I'm serious," she insisted. "It's been a difficult year and things are finally starting to look up. I heard on the news yesterday the Midwest is fallout-free, as long as we steer clear of the Detroit and Chicago hotspots. We could take a road trip to Jefferson City. Let the kids watch history being made."

As ridiculous as the idea had seemed to him at first, the more she talked the more sense she made. Society had been piecing itself back together around them, thanks in large part to the missionaries who had shown up from coast to coast. With their help, electrical power had been restored to Michigan's Upper Peninsula. Homes had running water again, and flushing toilets. Even the roadways had been cleared enough trade had started up again, if only for essentials like food and medical supplies. A tanker truck had come in last month and refilled both gas stations in town; David had worked enough hours with the rebuilding crews over the past six months to fill his tank and enough cans to last them there and back. Marilyn had put in more than her fair share of hours at the hospital, too, and even the kids had been helping out where they could. The whole family could probably use the break.

None of these were the main reason Marilyn wanted to go to Jefferson City, though, David knew. Last week—on the one-year anniversary of the fateful divisive election between Santos and Shepherd—there'd been a channel-wide broadcast on the newly-revived national television system. The religious, political, and military leaders who had guided them through the crisis had made official what everyone had known in their hearts since the first bomb fell: the United States of America was no more. Instead, they declared, a new nation would be founded in its place, one built on the principles of religious and personal freedom for every citizen. Its new name would be the United States of Believers. Those leaders had spent the past week in the Missouri State Capitol building, drafting the new nation's constitution. There was no telling how long it would take—none of the updates since had said anything about a timeline—but it would be something to remember the rest of their lives, to be there in person when the constitution was unveiled for the very first time.

The logistics of a vacation were a bit trickier to arrange than they'd been before the fall, but after a quick raid of the old AAA building in town and a few phone calls they had two rooms in a Jefferson City bed and breakfast for five nights. The last two, the proprietor told him; apparently the Chandlers weren't the only ones who'd decided to visit the new capitol. They even got stuck in traffic on I-54 into the city. A year ago David would've been annoyed, flicking through the radio stations for news while the kids griped in the backseat. Today, he and Marilyn just grinned at each other, oddly reassured by the normalcy of it.

As much as things had improved all over the country, Jefferson City felt like a different world. There were no visible signs of the destruction—a few empty storefronts, here and there, but even most of those had work crews bustling around inside, preparing them for new tenants. The Chandlers spent their first two days in town feeling like true tourists, wandering around museums and antique malls, eating in restaurants whose menus were pared down but still luxurious to them, their first time eating out since the disaster with the exception of church potlucks. Wherever they meandered, though, they were inevitably drawn back to the Capitol building, where they'd mingle into the small crowd that seemed to always be gathered outside the gate. David wouldn't be surprised if the building had received more visitors in the two weeks since closing than it ever did when it was open to the public, even in the old times.

Their second night in town, David and Marilyn left the kids in the room watching TV and made their way across the street to a little pub they'd seen the night before. The bars in their part of Michigan still hadn't re-opened, and while neither of them was a big drinker they both missed the camaraderie of a watering hole. It looked like a pretty standard dive when they walked in, dim and somewhat dingy but with a friendly vibe, the murmur of conversation layered over the country music playing on the jukebox and the sharp smack of balls striking each other on the pool table David could just see at the far back of the narrow space. He and Marilyn found two seats at the bar and ordered beers, almost overwhelmed by how casually the locals sat there socializing. He hadn't realized there were cities where life had picked up to this level of normalcy and it was heartening. Maybe this return to prosperity would spread throughout the new US of B once the new government began its work.

A news report came on the TV behind the bar, talking about the Second Constitutional Convention, even though there was no new information.

"Maybe they won't be done while we're here after all," Marilyn said.

"Unless you're leaving tonight, I wouldn't be worried," said the woman sitting in the stool on Marilyn's other side. When she saw their wary expressions, she smiled sheepishly and added, "Sorry for eavesdropping. Name's Pat Jacobs."

David and Marilyn introduced themselves. While David was shaking Pat's hand, he asked, "And what makes you so sure they'll be finished tomorrow?"

"I work with the new federal government," Pat answered. "Before the fall I ran an off the grid community down in Nevada. Once we heard what was being done here, how people were trying to rebuild society, we all made our way here to contribute our services. Not like I'm involved in the discussions or anything, but everyone who works at the Capitol building got a message today saying there'd be some big announcement happening at 10 tomorrow morning. I can't think of what else that would be."

Marilyn and David shared a look. Not a definite, but at least worth following up on. Not like they had any other plans for their time tomorrow morning. They chatted with Pat a bit more while they finished their drinks then headed back to the bed and breakfast, preparing for an early start the next day. As Pat had promised, the doors of the State Capitol building opened just after ten the next morning, and thanks to her tip the Chandlers were near the front of the crowd gathered to see it. The seven members of the new Presidential Council of the United States of Believers were introduced before the reading of their new constitution began. David felt tears spring to his eyes as they began to read the citizen rights. Tears of relief, he realized, that after all of this there might yet be a world left for his kids to grow up in. David squeezed Joe's shoulders, smiling to see his son looking so hopeful as the crowd around them erupted into cheers.

There'd been some debate at the Second Constitutional Convention about their policy on foreign affairs. Some argued for a completely isolationist approach, at least for the first few years, a chance for them to rebuild in peace, to avoid the influence of foreign powers. But there was no room for that kind of policy under the new World Government, apparently. The same day the new United States of Believers was officially christened, they were contacted by the United Nations and told to send a representative to participate in the final decision making stages. It was phrased as a request but there was an unspoken threat beneath the words. How could a new nation like the United States of Believers hope to survive without the assistance of this new world government? Perhaps they could rebuild without foreign aid but it would be a lengthy process, with no guarantee of success.

Two days later, their delegation boarded one of the nation's few remaining functional planes and was on its way to Paris. Since she was not one of the nation's leaders under the new constitution—a responsibility she was more than happy to have lifted from her shoulders, after the trials of the past few months—Carol Moore had been an easy choice to represent the United States of Believers in the World Government. Most of the policies of the new system had already been determined, but they would at least have a vote in the upcoming election of the first World President. A decision Moore wasn't exactly thrilled to be involved in. The field had already been whittled down to five candidates, but as she reviewed their profiles and experience in her Paris hotel room, Moore found she had misgivings about all of them. The current front-runner was the worst of the bunch. His name was Omar Masry and he was running on a platform that was blatantly anti-religion, pointing to religion as the source of all the world's conflict and violence. His bitterness against religion seemed to have personal roots; Masry had been badly injured while fighting for the Palestinian army in one of their many conflicts with Israel, an experience which, by his own admission, had led him to denounce God and all religion. He'd risen to prominence as the man who'd orchestrated the 2026 Treaty of Jerusalem, which had brought peace to the Middle East, something many had long thought would be impossible. Ironically, given his opposition to religion, his followers were near-fanatical in their support, seeming to worship him like some kind of surrogate for the God they claimed didn't exist.

Moore put down the reports on the candidates and sagged back in her seat, rubbing her eyes. Omar Masry definitely didn't seem like he'd be sympathetic to a nation whose leadership council contained five former religious leaders. But none of the other four had his support or qualifications. Did she really want the United States of Believers' first play on the international stage to be leading an opposition that was likely doomed to fail?

Moore opened her eyes and glanced over at the guard by her hotel room door. She'd almost forgotten he was there, he was standing so quietly. Moore smiled at him and asked, "What's your name, soldier?"

He seemed startled at first, like he wasn't sure she was talking to him, but then cleared his throat and told her, "Blake Davis, Ma'am."

"Have you been in the service long, Blake?" Moore asked.

"Not long at all," he answered. "Just signed up to help after the Chinese attacked. After the cease fire the new Army was looking for people to officially enlist and I thought, why not? I used to live in Oregon, so wasn't like I could go back home."

Moore asked, "What did you do before?"

Blake chuckled in a way that said he was laughing at himself. "Not much, honestly. I'd just gotten out of prison. I was arrested a few years back at a protest that turned violent."

"For which side?" Moore asked.

Blake smirked. "The other one."

Moore smiled herself. In the months before the election hearing him say he'd been a protestor for the left would have made her doubt her safety, wonder if she could trust him. Now, though, it was enough to know he'd put his life on the line defending the country. They'd finally been able to leave those political divisions behind them. Maybe the one positive thing to come out of all this destruction.

"What do you think about this whole World Government, Blake?" Moore asked, turning her eyes back to the profiles on the table.

"I'm not sure I'm qualified to answer that, Ma'am," Blake said. "But I do think I've seen more than enough fighting for my lifetime. If there's any way to make sure there's never a war like that again, well, I think it's at least worth giving it a shot."

Omar Masry had brought peace; Moore could say that much about him. It wasn't enough to win him her vote, but it was somewhat reassuring as she flipped through the other profiles, trying to decide which losing cause to back.

CHAPTER 18

OMAR MASRY HAD BEEN THE FRONT-RUNNER IN THE RACE for
World President since the end of 2033. With the election in early March,
it became official. Over the past year, the initial infrastructure of the
world government had been put into place. Control of militaries built by
individual nations had been turned over to a central authority, their resources pooled; troops from well-armed nations like Russia and China
were already being redistributed to nations like the United States of Believers, filling holes in their security forces and bolstering the efforts of
the remaining national guard. Many among the nation's leadership were
nervous at the thought of welcoming more foreign troops to their soil,
considering what had happened the last time they accepted so-called humanitarian aid. But they were in no position to resist, and the troops that
arrived lived up to the promise to help without interfering. They could
only hope Masry's leadership turned out to be equally beneficial. After
all, they told themselves in the United States of Believers—and other
world nations with religious leadership—he had always been an advocate
for peace.

Two weeks after his election, Masry took to airwaves around the world
to give his first State of the World address. His speech began innocently
enough, looking forward to the future and the bold new step the World

Government represented. When he shifted to policy, however, his words took on an ominous edge in the minds of believers.

"The world is at peace today," Masry said. "That has rarely been true in our planet's history. For most of human history, violence has been the rule and peace the exception. And at a root of an alarming number of those conflicts you'll find the same thing: religion. Fanatical belief in one god or another has prevented the world's citizens from seeing each other as brothers, dividing us into tribes that are always at odds. Countless wars have begun over the conflict of one religion with another. If we want war to become a thing of the past, so too must we purge the influence of religion from our institutions."

Masry paused then, looking out over the audience from his podium, the camera panning out to follow his gaze. Some were nodding along to his words, perched forward intently; others seemed concerned, their faces set into slight frowns, anxious lines around their eyes even if their expressions were otherwise blank.

The camera returned to Masry's face as he continued, "To that end, I am forming the new Department of Rational Government. Advisors from this department will be assigned to meet with the leaders of each nation. Their laws and leadership will be reviewed and assessed for religious influence. The Department will work together with these nations to remove these harmful influences from their policies. Together, we will preserve peace. We will no longer allow religious fanaticism to drive us to hatred and violence. Together, we will free ourselves from its damaging influence on our world."

There was more to Masry's address. He addressed the economy, the use of their new world troops, a council to bring more equality to the world's food supply; when he finished, the audience rose to their feet, thunderous in their applause.

"You can't tell me they're all really supporting this," Nate Wilson said, gesturing at the TV behind the bar. "I mean, it's not like we're the only ones who have religion baked into our culture. Italy, most of South America—I mean, come on, what's Vatican City supposed to do, here?"

Pat Jacobs sipped her beer and let Nate rant himself out. When he'd first shown up at her community, Pat had found Nate a bit annoying. She agreed with most of what he said but he was so aggressive about it. He had an opinion about everything and was never afraid to share it, even if nobody else was interested in hearing it. Over the months of their friendship, she'd both come to appreciate his passion—and learned how to tune him out when he started going on too long.

Nate wound down and took a chug from his own beer. Pat jumped into his silence to say, "He wouldn't have people there watching if he thought they'd disagree."

"But why would anyone agree with…that?" Nate shook his head and gestured to the bartender for another round.

"I'm a bit surprised to hear you have this take on things, to be honest," Pat said. "Weren't you just criticizing the new social policies the government just rolled out? I think your exact phrasing was that they 'reeked of socialism', if I remember right."

Nate said, "don't always like their policies, but that doesn't mean they shouldn't exist. We'd still be living in a wasteland, clusters of survivors fighting it out over the scraps, if the missionaries hadn't come to help us when they did. And it's a bad precedent if nothing else. If he's swooping in from the start to cut out religious rights, what's next? How many rights is he going to ask us to give up for peace?"

Pat didn't disagree with him. She'd fallen out of the habit of regularly attending church while she lived in her Nevada community but she'd always taken comfort in her faith, cherished her memories of attending services with her family as a child. She hadn't liked the idea of a world government from the start, to be honest—the national and state governments of the old US had been bad enough in their overreach, and a world government would only feel more justified—but she'd held out a hope before tonight that it would prove her wrong.

The door of the bar chimed. Pat turned as a pair of officers in the all-black World Forces uniform stepped in. They took a lingering look over the other patrons in the bar as they walked to an empty booth along the wall. One of Nate's coworkers, Blake, came in a second later, frowning at the pair in uniform as he took the empty stool on Pat's other side. As a one-time member of the radical left, he was especially distrustful of the World Force troops.

"Those guys give me the creeps," Blake muttered. "They say they're here to help but…"

He trailed off as the bartender arrived with Nate's next round, ordering a beer of his own before asking Pat, "Did I miss the whole speech?"

"Wrapped up a few minutes ago," Pat answered.

"Shoot," Blake said. "Well what'd I miss? Anything big?"

Pat chuckled as she slid off her seat. "Think Nate's the best one to fill you in on that. I'm gonna hit the restroom while you two talk it out."

Nate was already starting into the highlights behind her as she walked past the pair of World Forces officers. They were speaking loud enough to hear, though not in English; Russian, Pat thought, though she couldn't tell for sure. She tried to tell herself, again, that they were here to help, but with President Masry's words echoing in her mind she couldn't help wondering if that was all they were here for.

David Chandler woke up before dawn on Palm Sunday. He'd been inspired by his vacation in Jefferson City to take a more active role in local politics, and in the United States of Believers that meant first getting involved in the church. Their new government had done away with the old kind of politicians. The people put in charge in their new nation were those who had dedicated the most time in service to their community, and that was something David was more than willing to put his energy into. He was heading to the church now to help set up the community breakfast that would be served after the service. And he'd be there most of the day; after the breakfast, he was meeting with the local Bishop and a few other citizens to discuss their plans for a community garden next to the newly-reopened library. David chuckled to himself; these days, his schedule was just as busy as it had been before the fall. But it was different, now, the work he was doing. He wasn't just earning a paycheck; he was helping to rebuild society. That was work he could truly pour himself into.

It was a cool, foggy morning, and David drove slowly, watching for any of the deer whose population had exploded in the relative absence of people. Between the lingering fog and his attention to the road, he was already pulling into the church parking lot before he saw the black vans. There were three of them, pulled in a line along the edge of the parking lot by the door. David parked and hopped out, reaching the church entrance just as two black-uniformed World Force officers led the local Bishop out toward the vans in handcuffs, three more emerging and closing the church doors behind them.

"What's going on?" David asked, looking closely at the officers' faces under their helmets. Maybe they were locals and this was some kind of prank. But they were strangers, and they didn't look like they were joking.

"This church is closed," one of the officers by the door answered.

"But it's Palm Sunday," David protested. "And the community breakfast is going to happen here in a few hours. There are people in town that don't have a lot. They depend on that food."

"You'll have to find another venue," the officer replied.

Another added, "Community service events must be separate from any religious institution or influence. That's the new world law."

"And what about him?" David asked, gesturing at the Bishop. "Where are you taking him?"

An officer answered, "Questioning and re-education. It's a mandatory process for all religious leaders under the new world law."

"I'd suggest you head on home unless you want to go with him," another officer added.

David had never heard of any of these laws, but what could he do to fight? He was outnumbered and they were armed—heavily, by the looks of things. He watched, helpless, as they loaded the Bishop into the van and strung a padlock through the church doors.

"We have made great strides in the global fight against the tyranny of religion," Omar Masry said in his next world address. "It has been ninety days since I took office, and in that time there have been no armed conflicts between nations. There has been no war. All of those who have opposed the Department of Rational Government need only look at this fact to see the wisdom of my actions. I am the only Messiah the modern world needs, and I will bring the salvation humanity has sought from their false gods for too long."

He paused for the audience's applause, though the camera stayed focused on him, a tight shot of his face as he smiled over the crowd and said, "But religion is only one enemy of peace. Poverty and inequality are equally damaging to our ability to live as a global community. My next initiative will address this issue head-on by establishing a new global economy. In preparation for this, members of the World Forces will be setting up stations in all nations to implant each citizen with a bio-metric chip. Once this system is in place, the world government will be able to properly redistribute the world's resources. In the world I will build, no one will die of starvation or exposure while others hoard billions in their towers of privilege. In this new world, we will all be equal."

The applause in this pause was more scattered, undercut by anxious murmurs. The camera's eye never wavered, holding it's focus on Omar Masry's, the glare of the spotlights giving his eyes a feverish intensity as he outlined his plan for the New World Order.

www.ingramcontent.com/pod-product-compliance
Lightning Source LLC
Chambersburg PA
CBHW070718250726
48662CB00001B/471